THE FUTURE
OF THE WORLD

Western, Japanese
and Korean professors
participating
in the tour

THE FUTURE
OF THE WORLD

Scholars view the thought
of Reverend Moon

Edited by
Andrew Wilson, Ph.D.

This book consists of essays presented in Korea and
Japan in the summer of 1986 as part of a program
sponsored by the Advisory Council to the Unification
Movement International (ACUMI). ACUMI promotes
the involvement of scholars in the constructive
appraisal of the activities of the Unification
movement. ACUMI is a joint project of the
International Cultural Foundation and the
International Religious Foundation.

Published in the United States by the
International Cultural Foundation and the
International Religious Foundation
481 Eighth Avenue
New York, NY 10001

Produced by Vertizon, Inc.
1271 Broadway
New York, NY 10001

Designed by Jean-Francois Moulinet

ISBN 0-937301-01-9

Printed in the United States of America

Preface

The speeches collected in this volume record what was said in a very unusual lecture tour. In July 1986, thirty professors from America and Europe traveled throughout Korea and Japan, visiting gatherings in every city and province, to speak about the thought of the Reverend Sun Myung Moon and the impact in the West of the movement which he has created. In Korea they were joined by twenty Japanese professors and fifty Korean professors. Working in pairs consisting of one Western or Japanese professor and one Korean professor who both spoke and served as translator, they spoke at over 200 locations in four days. In Japan there were over fifty gatherings, each one graced by speeches from one Western professor, one Korean professor and one Japanese professor.

The purpose of this tour was to acquaint the people of Korea and Japan with the thought and work of the Reverend Moon and the Unification Movement. Although Korea is the birthplace of the movement—the Reverend Moon founded the Unification Church there in 1954—it was beset by persecution, particularly from Fundamentalist Christians who had considerable influence in Korean society. Reverend Moon always intended to create an international movement, and in late 1971 he came to America in order to realize his global vision. In the last decade and a half, the movement in the West has expanded and developed diverse activities: it has promoted a value-centered, internationalist vision for scholars through the International Conference on the Unity of the Sciences (ICUS), the Professors World Peace Academy (PWPA), and *The World & I* magazine; it has fostered ecumenism and interreligious dialogue through New ERA, the Assembly of World's Religions, the Religious Youth Service and the many projects of the International Religious Foundation (IRF), and it has come to the forefront of the ideological struggle against Marxism-Leninism through CAUSA and its sponsorship of the publications including the *Washington Times, The New York City Tribune,* and *Insight* magazine. Meanwhile, by comparison, the Unification Church in Korea has been neglected. Koreans have by and large not been touched by the international vision of the Reverend Moon, nor are they aware of the many activities he has inspired and the extent of his influence around the world.

That a religious leader might find more acceptance in distant lands than in his native country is not surprising. Jesus is recorded to have said, "A prophet is not without honor except in his own country." Jesus himself was ridiculed by his relatives and neighbors in the village of Nazareth, people who had known him from his childhood and could not believe that an apparently ordinary neighbor could be doing such great works. Indeed, Christianity took root not among Jesus' fellow Jews, but in the Hellenistic culture of the Roman empire. This has been the typical experience of religions and religious founders: Confucius wandered from state to state before he found a ruler who would adopt his principles, Muhammad encountered persecution in his native Mecca and only found acceptance during his exile at Medina, and Buddhism was harassed and finally wiped out from the Gautama's homeland of India but took root in China and Southeast Asia. The Unification Movement has likewise developed for the past decade and a

half in exile, in a Western environment far from its Korean roots. Yet, through this lecture tour, the Reverend Moon's thought and work could once again be presented to the Korean people.

Reverend Moon's vision is to create a new world culture uniting the best of Eastern and Western thought and society. While he always intended to develop a movement in the West to show the West its mission in the world, he from the outset has desired to see Korea transformed, and on that basis, to inherit the best of Western civilization as a complement to its Eastern traditions. Korea should then be able to serve as a model for the rest of the world. That Korea did not accept the movement nor benefit from its transforming vision has long been a cause of regret for the Reverend Moon. Now that Korea is opening to the West in its efforts to become an economic power, the Reverend Moon's thought has renewed relevance. The benefits of Western technology bring with them the mixed blessing of Western culture; the importation of consumerism and the commercial ideology of individualism and self-fulfillment can have drastic effects on a culture whose center has been family loyalties and an internal perspective on life fostered by centuries of Confucianism and Buddhism. Unificationism's religious principles of global harmony, which combine interior spirituality and the ideal of love in the family with an affirmation of science and technology, would help Korea assimilate the best of Western culture without compromising its moral and familial strengths.

Japan is another country where Eastern traditions are currently confronting Western culture and values. There the

Unification Movement has been quite successful, overcoming ingrained Japanese prejudice against Korea and things Korean on its way to gaining prominence in the academic and political fields. Yet as was the case with Korea, the Unification Movement in Japan has grown up in relative isolation from the Reverend Moon's work to develop activities in the West. Through this lecture tour, the Japanese Unification Movement could be instructed by the international vision of the movement as it has developed in the rest of the world.

The Japanese people have long been accustomed to cultural isolation, and they have clung to a narrowly nationalistic outlook even as they conquered international markets with considerable acumen. Yet many thoughtful Japanese realize that this attitude cannot continue, for at least two reasons. First, Japanese society has not been able to absorb Western technology without severe cultural strain, particularly as its young people have adopted Western cultural attitudes destructive to traditional Japanese mores. Second, Japan's economic preeminence has forced its leaders to ponder its responsibilities to the world community of nations. Faced with international discontent over its trade policies and the memory of its disastrous bid for leadership in Asia that precipitated its entry into the Second World War, the Japanese find that they lack the internal ideological basis to upon which they can found Japan's role as a world leader. For these reasons, leaders in Japanese society welcomed the lecture tour with considerable interest. The global religious vision of the Unification Movement may be of particular benefit in Japan's quest to realize harmony within its culture and a new

sense of political purpose in the international arena.

The scholars who have contributed to this volume have each had long association with one or another of the projects of the Unification Movement in the West. They became involved because they saw in these projects an expression of ideas which they themselves believed, and which they may have felt were not being adequately addressed by existing academic or professional institutions. While many first approached an offer to participate in one of the movement's academic or professional activities with some skepticism, they each became convinced of the activity's integrity and value, so much so that they have by and large willingly endured any criticism they have received from their colleagues. Through their association with the movement they have found a quality of professional interaction, often refreshingly cross-disciplinary and international, that has enriched their scholarship as well as their personal life, and improved their work in their own fields.

The thirty speeches in this volume come from scholars representing a broad spectrum of the movement's activities. They have been organized into seven groups: (1) those which give an overview of Reverend Moon's thought, especially its religious basis and its view of God and the family; (2) those in which scholars discuss their involvement in and hopes for the movement's ecumenical and interfaith activities; (3) essays concerned with the unity of science and technology with spiritual values and the challenge of bringing values into the arenas of public policy; (4) speeches describing the Reverend Moon's efforts to strengthen democratic values and institutions; (5) those concerned with his activities to promote peace and justice on a global scale; (6) those by scholars who consider Leninist communism to be a most serious threat to world peace and who support the Reverend Moon's educational and political activities to organize and disseminate a superior ideological position; and (7) statements describing the scholars' personal experiences with the Reverend Moon and expressing convictions which they have gained through working on these various projects. In an appendix is a paper by a noted Japanese biologist who describes how his mind was changed upon hearing one of the speeches of this lecture tour.

The reader is asked to excuse a certain amount of redundancy in these speeches, recalling that they were given to separate audiences — no audience heard more than one speech by a Western professor — so that many of the speakers felt an obligation to describe a general overview of what he or she knew of the movement's activities. On the other hand, neither should it be inferred that the professors whose speeches are printed herein have uniform opinions on all the diverse issues which one or another of them might have chosen to address. In fact, some who have joined wholeheartedly into one of the movement's projects might in other circumstances not cooperate with those who work with other projects whose proponents are also represented in this volume. Nevertheless, whatever their religious or political differences, the participants on this speaking tour found a camaraderie and fellowship grounded in a vision of a harmonious and peaceful world centered on religious values — a vision which is being brought closer to reality by the efforts of the Reverend Sun Myung Moon.

Reverend Chung Hwan Kwak
November, 1986

ONE

THE RELIGIOUS BASIS OF THE REVEREND MOON'S THOUGHT

The Vision
of Reverend Moon

Joseph H. Fichter

The name of Reverend Sun Myung Moon is known almost universally. His church, which has been called a "world-transforming" religious movement, is represented by his spiritual children in more than one hundred countries. My personal attention was drawn to him and the Unification Church in 1965 by John Lofland's sociological report *The Doomsday Cult*. It was a curious book. The author did not take seriously the leader, Professor Young Oon Kim, or the first American members. He tried to be objective and neither praised nor condemned the Church, but he was sure that it would soon disappear. Since then the Church has been the object of attack in America, Europe and Asia, but it certainly has not disappeared.

Ten years later, in 1975, I had my first personal contact with members of the Church at an annual meeting of the International Conference on the Unity of the Sciences. Most of the young people I met at that time were converts from the Catholic Church. Ever since then I have been trying to understand why a Catholic would want to become a Moonie. Actually, I have developed a twofold interest in the Unification Church: As a professor of Sociology I am studying the manner in which the Church tries to combine the religious and familial institutions. As a Catholic clergyman I am analyzing the manner in which the ecumenical principles of the Second Vatican Council can be vitalized in the movement toward the unification of world Christianity.

Most of what I want to say in this discussion is already contained in my book, *The Holy Family of Father Moon*,[1] which grew out of my experiences with many members and leaders of the Church. I have lectured and written on the Unifi-

Father Fitcher
poses with a group
of Unification Church
and IFVOC members
after the speech

cation teachings about marriage and the family. I had the privilege of teaching a course on the Sociology of Religion at the Unification Theological Seminary in Barrytown. I interviewed many members of the Church from different countries and included some of them in my book, *Autobiographies of Conversion.*[2] I have been a participant in five meetings of the International Conference on the Unity of the Sciences, as well as in the Assembly of World Religions, and in doctrinal seminars at Acapulco, Barrytown, New York City, Puerto Rico, Quebec, and Tenerife.

While I am not an offical member of the Unification Church, and I have reservations about some of the doctrines, I consider myself a close relative of the "family," as the members call themselves. So it is with great respect and appreciation that I attempt to appraise the impact of Reverend Moon's thought and teaching on the contemporary world. I have chosen to discuss several categories of his influence as follows:

a) *Unification Morality* embraces the reform of personal behavior and of ethical social relations. Achieving the "first blessing" of union with God is the beginning of a godly society.

b) *Unified Family* attempts to reform the basic unit of the larger society. This focus on the God-centered marriage and family is a recognition that social concern and civil virtue begin in the home.

c) *Cross-cultural Solidarity* promises to foster harmony to remedy the most serious rifts in global humanity. It aims to remove the antagonism and discrimination between races and nations.

d) *Christian Unity* is the exemplification of the Church's title and purpose: the Unification of World Christianity. The movement promotes the ecumenical aspirations of the major Christian denominations.

e) *Anti-Communism* is aimed at the elimination of collective Satanism. Reverend Moon is convinced that Communism is the greatest organized obstacle to the restoration of world humankind to God.

These five channels of Unification activity must be seen as a single concentrated global thrust for a better world. They operate simultaneously, although some may move more slowly and others more rapidly; some more successfully, others less successfully. If we express them negatively we may see them as a unified movement against the persistent evils of the world: the selfishness of human beings, the disruption of family life, conflict between races and nations, the disunity among competing religions, and the threat to world peace in satanic communism. We are all affected in some manner, as individuals and as groups, by these evils. Reverend Moon is striving constantly to restore the world to wholeness.

Unification Morality

When the *Divine Principle* deals with the "providence of restoration," the basic aim is to remove human beings from sinfulness and restore them as children of God. To resist evil and to embrace virtue has been an admonition of all religious leaders at all times, but Reverend Moon seems most deeply disturbed by the moral decadence of modern society. He implores his spiritual children that they strive to be the "Abel type" of human being in relation to all other persons. The distinction between good and evil is exemplified in the Cain-Abel biblical relationship in which Cain represents all that is unacceptable to God, while Abel symbolizes all degrees of

goodness. But Abel cannot be self-righteous; he is responsible to win over and educate Cain: "Abel cannot come to God alone; he has the responsibility to bring Cain with him, to win him over, to show him the clearer way."[3]

Unification morality is often interpreted as though its only concern is with the immoral sexual behavior that gains headlines in the media. It is true that such licentiousness seems to be the prevalent news of the day. Pornography and obscenity are everywhere, in magazines and movies, in books and videocassettes. Sociologists see this wave of permissiveness as a product of contemporary social structures and values. In some instances the churches too have "relaxed" their values and doctrines to accomodate the behavior patterns and preferences of their adherents. The Unification Church is almost unique by its insistence on premarital celibacy and marital fidelity. The young recruits of the Church understand from the beginning that sinful sexual relations are absolutely forbidden. The strength of moral character expressed in chastity is preparatory to their own future parenthood.

The focus on sexuality sometimes ignores the fact that the morality taught by Reverend Moon encompasses the total life behavior of the Church members. The so-called Calvinist ethic of hard work, frugality, self-restraint, and "this-worldly" asceticism is apparent in the behavior of Moonies. Although they feel no shame in imitating the medieval pattern of mendicancy—fundraising through begging and selling—they do not intent to imitate the life of poverty embraced by St. Francis of Assisi. They readily share their goods with fellow Moonies but they do not pronounce a vow of poverty. They are generous to the underprivileged, the unfortunate and the needy, but they help to develop individual competence that will raise poor families out of their deprived status.

The Puritan ethics of the Moonies is exhibited in some behavior patterns and not in others. They participate in music, singing and group dancing, and in dramatic arts in general. On the other hand, they show great moderation in eating and drinking, especially in the use of alcoholic beverages. They are not doctrinaire prohibitionists; they recognize the social and personal evils of alcoholism and drug abuse. Their abstemious behavior is an example of the moral self-control of the virtuous person, and an example of the moral counter-culture, quite contrary of the contemporary youthful notion of self-indulgence.

The Unification drive for a wholesome society focuses on both personal and social morality based ultimately on the love of God. The message of Jesus Himself is applied here when we remember that the greatest commandment is to love and serve God, and the second is to love and serve our neighbors. These are fundamental and contain all the other commandements. If you keep those two commandments you will be virtuous and will obey all the divine law: You will not lie or cheat or do any other harm to people around you. This is the healthy level of spirituality and morality promoted by Reverend Moon.

Unified Family

The traditions of Confucianism which have been deeply imbedded in the Korean culture emphasize the importance of kinship and family. The Confucian philosophy blends with the Unification ecclesiology, with the intent to bind family, religion and society in an unbreakable web of personal relationships. In the Unification movement the God-centered family is not only sociologically essential, it is also the vehicle of salvation. The vocation of marriage is God's calling for the development of personal spirituality. There is little room for the lifelong celibate in the Unification lifestyle because it is through the production of blessed children that the Kingdom of God will be generated on this earth. In a sense, then, one's personal vocation transfers to society's vocation.

The God-centered family is not merely a nice slogan or a spiritual ideal recommended by the church leaders. It is the essential core of community among the faithful of the church. It is also a deeply motivated system for restoring marital fidelity and family stability in modern society. One need not be an expert moral theologian to recognize the notable shift that has been occurring in the marital and family values of modern society. Many secularists see this change as an expression of personal freedom, an opportunity for self-actualization. Spiritually sensitive people see it as a decline in personal morality as well as a disregard for community needs and values. In either case, these changing patterns of behavior reflect a significant restructuring of the family system that has long been integral to Western civilization.

In Western society the statistics on the breakdown of marriage and family are very discouraging. Approximately half of the marriages contracted at the present time are likely to end in divorce.

The so-called "one-parent family"—with the mother as the one parent—is increasing in numbers with the result that the children are not given the benefit of fatherly care. Within the Unification Church there may sometimes be a separation or divorce, but this is an unfortunate disruption of the ideal relationship between wife and husband. The church member learns from the beginning that his/her authentic vocation before God is the marriage blessing, which is meant to be a solemn bond lasting for eternity.

We are at a point in history when the concept of the individualistic nuclear family has been stretched to the limits. The survival of society demands a shift back to multi-generational type of kinship system that embraces grandparents, parents and grandchildren. Enemies of the Church who do not understand the Unificationist family philosophy claim that the Church alienates members from their parents and families. The fact is that the Church institutes a biological and sociological lineage that extends across the generations. The extended family is the kinship group in which all members and relatives maintain a permanent solidarity. There appears to be no other modern remedy for the disruptive tendencies of the nuclear family. Perhaps the Unification family will one day become the model for all marriages, religious or secular.

Cross-Cultural Solidarity
Reverend Moon is perceived world-wide as an apostle of international peace and harmony. Not only has he initiated and supported the Professors World Peace Academy, he has consistently invited, for conference and dialogue, academic and religious representatives from all

Father Fitcher confers with local organisers in Ma San, Korea nations on earth. Eastern people have been invited to Western meetings, and Westerners—many for the first time—were introduced to the people and cultures of Eastern countries. More important than anything else is the generous and unselfish motivation that promotes this unity among the different races and nations of the world. The purpose is to fulfill the will of God, who wants all His children to be joined in a global community of love.

Americans are very aware of the fact that the Unification message of Christianity came from the East, which reverses the traditional procession of missionaries from West to East. Professor Young Oon Kim was the first, in 1959, of a gradually increasing immigration of Unificationist Koreans and then of Japanese. This means that the integration of the Church members was not only religious, but also cultural and racial. The leaders of the Church knew from the beginning that not all foreigners are welcomed with open arms into the lands they visit. The cultural influence of Korea, the language and customs and even foodstuffs, had to be absorbed by the Caucasian converts to the Church. There was some talk among the members about the Koreanization of all aspects of social living, even while the Korean sisters and brothers were getting used to Western customs. It is quite clear that the Japanese members also had large influence in the formation of the American Church.

What should be noted is that intercultural solidarity is a deliberate plan of the Unification movement, and this is demonstrated dramatically in the matching ceremony of prospective marriage spouses. Inter-ethnic marriage between Caucasians of European ancestry has been going on for generations in America: Italians married Irish, French married Greeks, and national background became less important, but interracial marriage was something quite different.

Reverend Moon has seen the importance of unity across racial lines, and he is the only religious leader who deliberately encourages marriage between Blacks and Whites, Orientals and Westerners.

This promotion of racially mixed marriages has brought opposition from people who argue for the so-called "purity" of racial heritage. The fact is that interracial marriages are gradually and slowly increasing in the younger American population, and one can only guess whether Reverend Moon's doctrine has been an influence in this increase. There is no question that the division between the Blacks and Whites has been the most pervasive kind of social disunity. The cleavage between the races, and the discrimination against the Blacks, was the worst immorality in the history of the American society. The effort to remove this disgraceful system of injustice and discrimination from the American scene has been one of the most significant contributions of Reverend Moon and the Unification Church.

The internationalism of the Unification movement, which brings together the traditions of East and West, is a repudiation of European colonialism and of Asiatic imperialism. For more than four centuries there existed a system of suppression by European colonial powers that kept whole continents in subjugation. It is only in our lifetime that Mahatma Ghandi led the revolution that threw off this yoke. Revolutions have also freed the African and Asian countries from this colonial servitude.

The movement for equality and justice for the underprivileged peoples is elevated by the Unificationists to a movement of mutual and universal love.

Christian Unity

The fragmentation of Christianity into denominations that are often in opposition has been a sorry fact of Western society. In his well-known work on the *Social Sources of Denominationalism,* Richard Niebuhr called it a scandal; he said that "the history of schism has been a history of Christianity's defeat." This is a serious indictment for the Christian believer who knows the prayer that Jesus said the night before He died. He prayed that His followers "may all be one." Their unity was to be a demonstration to the world that they are the children of God, "so they may be completely one, in order that the world may know that You sent me and that You love them as You love me." (John 17:23)

Religious disunity has occurred in all periods of history and in all nations, but it is especially reprehensible among the followers of Jesus who proclaim themselves the children of God, the Father, and the siblings of God, the Son. We read in the *Divine Principle:* "What makes Christianity different from other religions is that its purpose is to restore the one great family which God had intended at the creation." (p.123) As everyone knows, the formal title of the Church is the Holy Spirit Association for the Unification of World Christianity. This is not a goal unique to Reverend Moon, since the same objective is announced by the World Council of Churches of Jesus Christ and by the celebrated Decree on Ecumenism, *Unitatis*

Redintegratio, of the Second Vatican Council.

There are different programs for ecumenical unity. In some, like the Roman Catholic approach, an invitation is extended by the parent church that the sectarian groups "come back home." More typical is the concept of federation, in which the member churches share theological doctrine but remain structurally autonomous. If I understand Reverend Moon correctly, he does not conceive of Christian world unification as the absorption of all other Christian Churches into the single universal church under one leadership and authority. He does not insist on "exclusive" membership but appears to encourage the Unification members to participate in the worship services of any and all other Christian churches.

Neither does Reverend Moon conceive of a structural system in which the various denominations share the same doctrines, rituals and polity. He wants to bypass all the debates and disputations about beliefs and practices that have fragmented the Christian Church in past centuries. He calls for a spiritual experience of divine and human love that can be shared among people even though they differ profoundly in their theology. It may be expressed in relatively simple terms in the hypothesis that "if you really love God, you must love all of God's children." Universal love, then, is the cement that holds all Christian believers together.

The Unification movement has also reached out to the representatives of world religions other than Christianity. The Assembly of World Religions was a deliberate effort to develop ecumenical understanding with Buddhists, Moslems and other founded religions. Concern for the relationship with non-Christian religions grows out of Unification Church's origins in the multi-religious society of Korea.

Anti-Communism

The life-style of the Unification members is in many respects communitarian and expresses itself in a voluntary sharing of this world's goods. In other words, they practice a kind of Christian socialism patterned on the manner in which the early disciples of Christ are described in the Acts of the Apostles. The whole church is geared to give assistance to the poor and underprivileged of the larger society. This is charity and philanthropy and social welfare on behalf of the needy, but it is balanced with an entrepreneurial spirit and practice upon which individuals may reach some degree of material success. In other words, their crusade against Communism is not a doctrinaire insistence on laissez-faire Capitalism.

It is a well established fact that the political influence of the Unification Church and its leader is a kind of far-right conservatism. Reverend Moon's declaration of loyalty to the American Presidency was demonstrated most clearly when he continued to support President Nixon even when he was on the verge of impeachment. He teaches his followers to be obedient to legitimate authority, whether democratic or monarchial. In other words, the Moonies are law-abiding citizens, not only in the avoidance of criminal activities, but also in the practice of civic virtues demonstrated in the loyalty of obedient citizens. It is this principle of citizenship that prevents the members from participating in protest meetings and marches against the government. As a matter of

fact, however, they are willing to demonstrate publicly on social and moral issues and especially against Communism.

The Moonie opposition to atheistic Communism gains the greatest publicity in the CAUSA movement, which sponsors conferences of clergymen frequently and in many American cities. Wherever possible these meetings are addressed by men and women who have had first-hand experience with Communists in Cuba, Poland, Eastern Europe, and elsewhere. CAUSA publications feature articles attacking Communism. It is well-known that Reverend Moon was a prisoner of the North Korean Communists even before he gathered his followers for the organization of the Holy Spirit Association. He fears the Communist threat to world peace. The Unification promotion of democracy has strong spiritual and political motivation.

Perhaps this opposition to Communism has its strongest motivation in moral and theological doctrines. Reverend Moon preaches regularly that Communism represents Satanism. He writes that Satan "is steering his way toward the world of communism by advocating so-called 'scientific socialism' based on materialism."[4] He is rigorously opposed to materialistic, atheistic socialism, which is Satanic Communism. On the other hand, the people of God naturally seek the benefits of a proper "socialistic system of life." The will of the people has to move in that direction; "therefore, there will ultimately have to come a socialistic society centered on God."[5]

The Unificationist goal is a world of spiritual and moral cooperation among people in all classes of society. The disruptive aspect of the Communist movement is that it pits class against class, bosses against workers, bourgeois against proletarian. The Communist world is a world of antagonism and dissatisfaction that can maintain an ongoing structure only through some form of collective dictatorship. It is probably safe to say that unless there is victory over Communism, all the other Unification goals would disappear: elevated ethical behavior; strong family life; genuine international love, and inspired religious ecumenism. Without these benefits it would indeed be a gray and sorry world.

Notes

1. Joseph Fichter, *The Holy Family of Father Moon,* (Kansas City: Leaven, 1985).

2. Joseph Fichter, *Autobiographies of Conversion,* (Lewiston: Edwin Mellen, in press).

3. Young Oon Kim, *Unification Theology and Christian Thought,* (New York: Golden Gate, 1975) p. 202.

4. *Divine Principle,* (Washington: HSA-UWC, 1973) p. 445.

5. *Ibid,* p. 444.

The Significance of Reverend Moon and the Unification Church for our World Today and Tomorrow

Osborne E. Scott

Ladies and Gentlemen,

This visit to Korea and Japan as a part of the Unification seminar on the contribution of Reverend Moon and the Unification Church to our world today and tomorrow is highly significant personally for me and my wife. We have deep roots both in Korea and Japan which go back to the days of the beginning of Reverend Moon's ministry here.

I came to Korea in 1953 as a member of the Armed Forces serving in the Second Infantry Division. We fought for the liberation of Korea. Toward the end of my tour in Korea in 1954 after the cessation of hostilities, my division engaged in the Armed Forces rehabilitation program to rebuild areas in which we were located. As deputy project officer for the Second Infantry Division, whose area extended from Kinsal in the North to Chung Chung in the East to the little village of Masoug-Ri about thirteen kilometers from Seoul, I was instrumental in planning and supervising the rebuilding of schools, dispensaries and churches in these areas. My division had already by the time of my arrival built and endowed an orphanage in Chung Chung and turned it over to the Catholic missionaries for operation.

While I was serving in Korea, my wife mobilized our city of Mount Vernon, New York to adopt the Korean village of Masoug-Ri. The Mayor of Mount Vernon issued a Proclamation of Adoption, the doctors gathered medical supplies, schools and children contributed school supplies and the general public and churches collected clothing. These were sent to Korea and distributed at an appropriate ceremony in Masoug-Ri.

My family joined me in Japan when I was reassigned from Korea and stationed at Camp Zama, near Tokyo, the headquarters of the U.S. Army in the Far East. My wife, as president of the United Church Women of Tokyo, had the opportunity to visit Korea in 1954 and see some of the rehabilitation work and experience the warmth of the people and children who welcomed them. We remember Dr. Helen Kim, president of Ewha University. The Ewha Choir sang at our Division Easter sunrise service in the Kumwa Valley in 1954. As you see, our roots do extend far back in time and we are pleased to return to Korea and Japan and renew our friendship. I have visited Korea several times since my early service here as a part of the Revisitation Program sponsored by the Korean government and the Korean Veterans Associations and as a participant in conferences sponsored by the Unification Church.

My first involvement with the Unification Church began when as a professor at the City College of New York, I had two Unification Church members as students in one of my classes. They were both excellent students, but what impressed me more was the sincere and enthusiastic devotion to their religion and the practical demonstration of their faith. I had a sense that they were not just giving lip-service to religion but were expressing their beliefs in their lives, often at the expense of opposition and pressures from fellow students. They exposed me to the Divine Principle and the theology of the Church but more than that, to an expression of love that seemed to be at the heart of what religion is really all about. Through their introduction, I became a sponsor of CARP, a student organization, on my campus. I entertained its members in my home and became a champion of their right to follow their religion.

I consider my relationship with the Unification Church an extension of a deep religious conviction which includes the right of all people to approach their God in their own way and the validity of all religions before God. Perhaps this statement taken from Dr. Anthony Wallace's book, *Religion: An Anthropological Study* is at the heart of my approach to religion and has been the basis of my view of the Unification Movement and new religions:

New religions are constantly being born. From the most ancient of archaeological records, from the history of the most recent past, and from the millenia in between, rises a ceaseless clamor of new faiths. Every year about the globe, dozens of new religious expressions (cults) add their voices to the cry. They are rarely faiths unique in doctrine and ritual; almost invariably they are composed for the most part of pieces and patterns of older, more routinized, more conservative religions. Their newness resides in the attitude of their membership. Their members, few or many, are once-disillusioned, easily inspired people who have forsaken the ways of the world about them and have banded together to build what they believe to be better selves and a better world. Rarely indulged by the old religions, the new are variously ignored, sneered at, or violently suppressed; a few survive, grow, and become old religions. But all old religions were new religions once.

If we understood the process by which new religions came into being we should be close to understanding other basic processes of human life... New religions have been the inexhaustible fountains from which for thousands of years have flowed, in turbulent variety of form and color, the waters which make up the sea of faith... That sea has nourished much of man's still infant culture—not merely his theological belief and sacred ritual, but his values, his principles of social organization, even his technology.

Dr. Osborne Scott

Dr. Wallace finds that periodically new religions reverse the course of decline by providing energy and direction for a new and often higher development. Religion according to anthropologists has a function of bringing about cultural change. Max Weber found that the Protestant ethic was a new value system suited to the development of capitalism in post-Renaissance Europe. Emile Durkheim, in his search for the origin of religion, proposed that the true object was to inculcate those values (aspirations) necessary to the society's survival. "The function of religion is to make people want to do what they have to do anyway."

There are six areas in which Reverend Moon's thinking and the Unification Movement have made a distinct impact on our world, our life and spiritual development. The first is an emphasis on *God* and his place in our lives, the second is the concept of the *family* and the oneness of the world's people, the third emphasizes *the unity of all religions,* the fourth is the belief in *absolute values,* the fifth is *the worth and dignity of all men* as members of the family of man, the last is *the role of the prophet* in bringing about change.

I. God
Unificationism has brought to us a renewed emphasis on God as Creator of the world and ruling force in our lives. It has taken him off the shelf where he had been conveniently placed and made him live again in our lives. Its emphasis on God has brought a new personification of him. He is the foundation on

which all theology and practical living rests. Unification prayers are like personal conversations and God described as having *heart*. One of the most stimulating series of conferences sponsored by the Church has been on "God: The Contemporary Discussion." I was privileged to have attended the first of these seminars. Here were gathered Christians of all denominations with Moslems, Hindus, Buddhists and other representatives to discuss the central figure in all of our religious lives. I felt the very presence of so many different religions and their sincere and scholarly discussion moved us beyond the limits of our faith and made us realize that we were approaching the same Being and discussing the highest in all religions, regardless of the name or terms we used for His name.

I would like to quote from a paper presented on Reverend Moon's teaching by Reverend Chung Hwan Kwak on "God and Creation in Unification Theology."

> How can we know God? As the unique and eternal first cause of everything, God cannot be confined within the space-time of this world. As the standard of perfection and the source of all ideals, God is absolute and unchanging. How can we, who live in a spatial-temporal and changeable world, know God, who is unique, absolute and unchanging..? We can know God because we are created in his image. Jesus taught us to call God "Father" and to love all human beings as our brothers and sisters. He cautions us that our own true happiness is to be found only in the Kingdom of God; and out of his love for God. His (Jesus') self sacrificial love manifested in an unwavering effort to lead us to true happiness, reflects the most essential aspect of God—what Unification theology calls "Heart." Heart is

the impulse to seek joy through loving someone or something. Heart manifests itself in love which is purposeful activity which serves, benefits and invigorates someone or something. As such, love involves intellect and will as well as emotion; so heart is deeper than intellect, emotion, and will and is the starting point and motivation for all three.

II. The Family

A second contribution of Reverend Moon and the Unification Movement is the emphasis on family. This naturally grows out of a concept of God as Father. The central structure for all our relationships is the family. Unificationists see themselves as being part of a family. They speak affectionately to each other as brother and sister and Reverend and Mrs. Moon as their "true parents." The place of the family has undergone severe strain, not only in the West but throughout the world. The concept of the family has entered a critical stage of disintegration. In the United States one of every three marriages ends in divorce. Our families have been torn apart with a devastating impact, particularly on our children. Many of our young people who heard Reverend Moon's emphasis on family were attracted to his message and joined the Unification family. The family is the heart of Unification relationships and could be the motivation for a reconstitution of the family in the broader secular world.

III. The Unity of Religion

A third contribution of Reverend Moon's thinking and the Unification Movement is the unity of religion. The very name "unification" implies one of the church's goals, the unification of world religions. Reverend Moon has invited us to look beyond the limits of our own religious differences which separate us. He has dared to bring together in all his conferences and seminars in fellowship and discussion representatives of all religions. Perhaps one of the most far-reaching programs is the Youth Seminar on World Religions, which each year takes representatives of many groups to the world's religious capitals to talk and learn from religious leaders. I have attended the discussion of these young people and have witnessed the deep insights and inspiration gained from this experience. Many expressed the feeling that their lives had been changed forever, and indeed they have.

This emphasis on the unity of religions has been a decisive contribution to mankind's movement from the state of tribalism to universalism. We are all on that path of development that could be greatly enhanced by this spirit.

IV. Absolute Values
In a world that has moved more and more to relativism, the emphasis on absolute values once again affirms that our world has a purpose, and that the structure of the eternal is absolute. His stimulating International Conference on the Unity of the Sciences has had as the main purpose the restating, analyzing and reinforcing of the concept of values as that structure which holds life together.

V. The Worth and Dignity of All Men
Perhaps the single most important contribution of Reverend Moon's influence on our world and certainly for me personally has been his emphasis on the worth and dignity of all men regardless of status, race, religion, nation or culture. When Reverend Moon was asked who in America was the greatest person in this century, he replied without hesitation, "Dr. Martin Luther King, Jr." He had recognized the greatness of this man who had stimulated the aspirations of millions and brought about changes vital to the recognition of the worth of all people.

This emphasis on the value of all men is not simply an academic or ideological concept. The Unification Movement practices it in the daily living of its members. I was privileged to attend the mass wedding of two thousand couples in the Madison Square Garden in New York City in 1982. I observed the procession of wedding couples as they moved from the World Mission Center to the Garden, about one city block along the main avenue to the area of the wedding. The mixture of couples, Asian, Western, African, Black and White, all nationalities and races, being joined together in the most fundamental of relationships was most impressive. I was particularly impressed with the bystanders, the police who were controlling the traffic and those who out of curiosity stopped to look. On their faces was written such expressions of amazement. They looked as if they had seen a vision of an "ideal world," the world as it could be.

VI. The Role of the Prophet
A final contribution which I wish to emphasize of Reverend Moon and the Unification movement which Reverend Moon has given by example, is an emphasis on the role of the prophet in bringing about social change.

When I was stationed in Japan in 1954, I attended a small group meeting of Asian students in Tokyo. At this meeting was a young Indonesian student, who came up to me seeing the cross of the chaplaincy on my uniform. He approached me with this statement, "The religion of my father is dead. It has nothing to say to us, the youth. Who and what are you, prophet, priest, or medicine man?"

I was caught up at the time, but his statement has lingered with me for these thirty years. Whenever I seek to reexamine myself, my profession and my religion, I ask myself again this question, Who am I, prophet, priest, or medicine man? We have some of each in us.

The medicine man is the manipulator. He uses his religion for his own ends, gives very little except in terms of his own personal achievement. The priest keeps the ritual and religious machinery moving. He is the performer. Most of us as ministers are priests of our religions.

The prophet is the one who moves religion and our world to new heights. He has been described as being most vulnerable. He exists in a "no-man's land." If we drew two circles, one representing the world as it is and the other the world as it could be (and must be) and make these circles overlap, the prophet exists in the area where the circles overlap. He is in the most difficult area of existence. He physically is in a world that is, but his heart, mind and soul lives in a world that is yet to be. He sees visions and dreams dreams. He is vulnerable because his thinking threatens that world which often rejects and

persecutes him. At times he must live only with his dreams. He disturbs the status quo, the accepted mores and practices and the complacent beliefs.

Jesus was a prophet, so was Mohammed and Buddha, and so is Reverend Moon. He is among those who dare see their mission as moving mankind to higher goals and new horizons. It is no mere accident that Reverend Moon has been persecuted, subjected to imprisonment, misunderstood. This is the life the prophet must expect and I am sure Reverend Moon does. When imprisoned he cautioned his followers to "love your enemies." He held no malice or hatred for those who had persecuted him. Jesus of Nazareth went to the cross. There is a cross for the prophet. In some respect this, too, is part of the role of religion in the revitalization process for mankind. It is part of God's plan.

The prophetic role is in some respect open to all of us. I heard one of our participants on this seminar, Dr. Herbert Richardson, state that when he asked Reverend Moon the question, "Are you the Messiah?" his reply was, "And you must be a Messiah, too."

Jesus of Nazareth stated it this way, "He that would save his life shall lose it. But he that loses his life for a higher world, the nobler cause, shall find it." He also said, "These things I do you shall do, and even greater things shall you do, because I go to the Father." Reverend Moon challenges us to be among those who commit themselves to doing "the greater things."

A Critical Appreciation of *Divine Principle*

Geddes MacGregor

Introduction

I wish to begin by expressing my deep appreciation to the Reverend Sun Myung Moon and the Unification Church not only for inviting me to give this lecture in Korea and Japan but for the many opportunities I have been so graciously provided in the past five years to participate in the diverse activities of the movement and especially for the opportunity of getting to know the warmth and friendship of many of the young people who are personally dedicated to its work.

My first such experience was at the Tenth ICUS, held in Seoul in the fall of 1981. I must confess that, when first invited there with almost no previous acquaintance with the movement, I went with considerable misgivings, not to say skepticism. My attitude was predictably critical and sometimes expressed in critical questions. What impressed me more than the magnificence of that especially large-scale international conference, even more too than the lavish and gracious hospitality of our host, was the readiness of the members of the Church not only to welcome such criticism but to seek it in order that they might express better the convictions of their hearts and minds. Such open-mindedness is, to say the least, both healthy and heart-warming.

At the root of Unificationist convictions lies a fundamental document: the *Divine Principle*, representing the revelation received by the Reverend Sun Myung Moon. The commission I received for the invitation to give the present lecture was to address myself to some of the key issues in that remarkable book and to deal with them both appreciatively and critically. I have

Dr. Geddes MacGregor
in Kagoshima, Japan

selected a few of what seem to me the most basic and provocative ones.

Before proceeding to the details of my task, it is useful, I think, to notice the bifurcated philosophical and theological roots of the Unificationist thought.

On the one hand are certain clearly Confucian elements to which I shall allude from time to time in the course of this lecture. Neither Oriental nor Occidental inquirers should overlook the significance or value of these. Confucius, as is well known, was both a practical and a deeply conservative thinker. What we call Confucianism contains, therefore, much ancient Chinese wisdom that long antedates the age of Confucius himself. Confucius, as is no less well recognized, did not purport to offer either a metaphysical philosophy such as can be found in Taoism or an analytical psychology such as may be seen in many forms of Buddhism. He was much more in the spirit of Socrates, his Occidental counterpart.

On the other hand, however, Unificationist thought has plainly been much influenced by Christianity in the very special form it takes in the kind of Presbyterianism that was notably represented in the Protestant Christianity exported to Korea. During the American occupation of South Korea (1945-1948) many American and other foreign missionaries had returned to Korea and had resumed activities hitherto proscribed. The first president, Mr. Syngman Rhee, was a Methodist and although the first vice-president, Mr. Shee Young Lee, was not a churchman, a later vice-president, Mr. Tai Young Hahm, was a Presbyterian minister. Many ministers of that denomination entered political life and were generally held, as were Christians generally, in high regard. Removal of former Japanese Government restrictions opened the way to the rapid Christianization of South Korea. In 1955, after the Korean War of 1950-53, there were thirty presbyteries of the Presbyterian Church, all located in South Korea. Presbyterianism was by no means, however, then a newcomer to Korea. It had been caught up as early as 1907 in a movement known as The Great Revival. In 1910 it had reached its climax in what came to be called "the Million Soul Movement": a campaign of co-operative activities in personal evangelism by all Protestant denominations. Although Methodist in origin, this movement owed much to Presbyterian influences. The Korean Presbyterian Church had joined the World Pan-Presbyterian Alliance about the same time as The Great Revival, and people were likening such events to the Pentecost as recorded in the second chapter of the Book of Acts.[1]

The effect of the liberation of religious activity in 1945 after the end of World War II can be easily imagined. It was like the explosive growth of a healthy but hitherto potbound tree. In near-strangulation from the annexation of Korea to Japan in 1910, Christianity in Korea thirty-five years later saw a new era of hitherto undreamt expansion, and in such an environment Presbyterianism in Korea grew notably. It is by no means surprising, therefore, that the Reverend Sun Myung Moon, growing up in Korea at a time when the Christian Church was both persecuted and profoundly influenced by certain theological ideas traditionally emphasized in the Presbyterian tradition, should reflect an emphasis of such ideas in his interpretation of those Christian elements that are so vigorously enunciated in the *Divine Principle.*

Divine Principle is indeed not only an original work; it is itself a unification of a profoundly wise Oriental mode of thought and a very special form of the many faces that Christianity has taken in the course of its very complex history. While appreciating its importance I propose to look critically and, I hope, constructively at a few of the central issues it presents.

The Nature of Man

Both Confucius and Socrates, his Occidental counterpart, recognized in their day that philosophy ought to begin with the study of man. As Alexander Pope was to put it nearer our own time:

Know then thyself, presume not God to scan;
The proper study of mankind is Man.

Unlike his fashionable sophistic contemporaries, Socrates was fundamentally religious in his outlook and disposition. He perceived the uniqueness of man that was to be expressed in the seventeenth century of our own era by Pascal as *la grandeur et la misère de l'homme:* man is, on the one hand, a beast, on the other hand an angel; he has one foot in the soil and another leaping up to heaven. Empirically we know of no entity to compare with him.

Divine Principle, in common with this stance, sees man as unique in this way, living in these two dimensions. Man cannot be made happy by the attainment of material blessings only; his nature is such that his happiness is unattainable without the attainment of a right relation with what is traditionally called in the Western tradition the *summum bonum,* which is the chief end of man and may be called God.

Since man is a being with a "spiritual" as well as a "material" nature, one would expect that in his quest for happiness he would always choose to seek whatever is good for his "spiritual" side and is conducive to the attainment of his happiness in that dimension of his being. One would expect that, as even the lowest forms of life instinctively know what is good for them to eat and how to best avoid danger, man would know what is right and good for him to pursue and would eschew instinctively what is contrary to his spiritual interests. Confucius believed, as did Socrates too in his way, that but for ignorance man could not but choose the right. So indeed it would be, according to the *Divine Principle*, but for the "Fall". Here Unificationists borrow the traditional symbolism of Christian theology to express the truth that a mysterious discrepancy exists between what we would do if we were wholly rational and what in fact we do do. In one way or another we are not what we ought to be. We may say (as in the Calvinist tradition) that we have inherited a moral disease that impedes what ought to be our natural propensity to do the will of God, since that must be as surely our highest interest as it is a worm's highest interest to protect itself by burrowing and disappearing into the ground whenever it "sees" a shadow hovering over it. We are indeed half angel, half beast.

I would suggest that it is important to recognize the symbolic character of the great truth to be found in the traditional teaching of the Fall. Traditionally, there was no way of understanding it except as in some sense a past event that somehow or other occurred in time. For the ancients did not understand the evolutionary character of the universe; nor indeed did anyone properly understand it till the nineteenth century. So the truth in the concept of the Fall could hardly be seen otherwise than as a past event. Man *had had* a perfect nature which he *lost*. But what if he had not yet attained the capacity to reconcile his "material" or "lower" aspect with this "spiritual" or "higher" one? What if he were on the way to attaining this harmony but had not attained it and might take a very long time in the process of doing so? If, as now seems plain, the evolution of biological life on our planet has already taken billions of years, man's attainment of the harmony that he needs (to overcome the tension that all the religions detect in him) is certainly not to be expected to come about overnight.

Creation

That man, no less than the rest of the universe, is in some way created by God is taught very widely in the great religions. For historic reasons, however, creation has been much misinterpreted. The notion itself is crucially important, for adherence to some sort of doctrine of creation is what separates the outlook of those whose God-centered view of everything precludes their resting content with any notion of a universe in which all things simply emerge and grow, ungoverned by any principle and devoid of any cosmic purpose. But we must examine what creation as a doctrine entails. The notion that it took place as a past event entails the view that God was perfectly and eternally happy alone by himself and that He then created it with all the appurtenances of time and space that were needed for the new adventure. This is what a literalistic reading of Genesis would lead one to suppose. It is a radically absurd view. Nor is it warranted by the Hebrew text, since in Hebrew the tense-structure is such that the word used for what is translated "created" does not at all have the implication of "past-ness" that the translations into Greek, Latin, and other languages generally suggest. The Hebrew is compatible with the view that God creates eternally, since that is in effect his *métier*, that is what it means to be God the Creator. So creation must be an ongoing activity, unless we are to say that things just somehow fall into place by themselves. Even in the Septuagint, (that most important Greek version of the Scriptures, which the New Testament writers themselves used) we have a hint, to say the least, that this understanding of creation as eternally ongoing is what is intended, for the first verse begins with the word *en archē*, that is, not "in the beginning" in the sense of "when time began" or "before anything else occurred" but rather, as we might express it today, "archetypally": a very different concept indeed.

Man is in the midst of a vast creative process: a slice indeed of nature; but what an interesting slice! We are not all at the same place in the slice, but we are all part of the same divine process and all endowed with the same capacity for the achievement of freedom: a topic to be discussed later.

God the Creator can be conceived, however, in various ways. Aristotle, in a stroke of philosophical genius, saw him as First and Final Cause: a magnet drawing all things to Himself. Yet Aristotle's preoccupations made it possible for him to remain content with the notion of God as an intellectual principle without heart, without the kind of love that is attributed to him in the biblical and other traditions that are deeply religious in outlook. Unificationists properly see God as endowed not only with the highest intellectual activity but also as acting always in love and out of a uniquely holy love for His created universe. This Unificationist doctrine has affinities with the Catholic doctrine of the Sacred Heart: a doctrine and a devotion developed only in comparatively recent centuries by the Carthusians and then of course in a more popular form, although in somewhat unfortunate iconography, as a result of the visions of Margaret Mary Alacoque.

The notion proposed in the Gospels, then, that not a sparrow falls to the ground without our Heavenly Father's knowing it and caring about it, is an essential aspect of any view of God's attitude toward His creation that is to take into account the full nature of God, which is to be considered later.

Creation must be seen as the *characteristic* activity of God or else not at all.

"Science" and Religion

There is, of course, no such thing as "science" as popularly conceived. There are only sciences. All use, however, methodologies that have many common features.

The "war" between science and religion is by no means a modern one only. It was in full swing, for example, in the thirteenth century, when Thomas Aquinas attempted, with extraordinary success in terms of his day, to reconcile the then traditional intellectual outlook of the Church with the newly developing challenge of "science," which happened to take the form of Aristotle as then recently rediscovered in the Latin West. Aristotle *was* science.

Thomas Aquinas was at heart a Platonist, but with a strong sense that truth must be one and that in the long run there could be no fundamental incompatibility between "science" and religion. No doubt to his surprise, as he sought to meet the challenge of his day on this arena, he perceived that, properly understood, Aristotle and the Bible were not at all the foes they seemed to many to be. On the contrary, he found that in many cases they were astonishingly easy to reconcile. Where they were not, or seemed not to be, the difficulty lay in what Thomas accounted the shortcomings of reason contradistinguished from revelation. He had an immense respect for the claims of reason. So when, for example, Aristotle held that God must be eternally creating, Thomas claimed that, while this was precisely what a good philosopher ought to conclude, it happened not to be the case, since God had revealed otherwise in Genesis. That Thomas was wrong in his interpretation of Genesis is a fact that we must recognize as inevitable in a thinker of his time. That he could see that the universe itself is revealed to us even in nature always comes to us as a surprise (why should we expect, from any *a priori* principle, that oak leaves should have the shape they have or that kangaroos should exist at all?) shows his extraordinarily acute philosophical imagination and acumen.

In Aquinas' day the notion of inductive logic and methodology had been little if at all developed. The men of the later Middle Ages were astonishingly clever in their use of technology; nevertheless, they were hampered by lack of understanding of the way in which scientific truths and principles are to be discovered.

The division of human inquiry into the "natural" sciences on the one hand and, on the other, the philosophical, humanistic and theological sciences is a comparatively modern one. The early Greek thinkers, for example, made no such distinction. They simply inquired about "the nature of all things," so that one may call them either primitive scientists or primitive theologians as one pleases. The Bible also is innocent of such a distinction. The Hebrews, having no word for nature, simply attributed to God the phenomena we would attribute to nature: earthquakes and thunderstorms are directly due to divine activity. What, then, brought about the change that made the now familiar division seem necessary?

The word "science" means simply "knowledge" or "learning" (Latin, *scientia,* from *scire* to know). As the pursuit of knowledge followed more than one path, however, people began to perceive a basic difference between the way that mathematicians and physicists, on the one hand, and humanists and theologians, on the other, pursued their respective goals. In the Arab world, which in the ninth century of our era, before the rise of the great universities in Europe, was the undisputed custodian of what would nowadays be recognized as scientific learning, the difference grew to seem sharp. For how could one discern truth when the physicists said one thing and the Qur'an another? How could one prefer the one over the other, since the evidence of the former seemed indisputable and the authority of the latter irrefutable except by infidels? Some, in this difficult situation, proposed, in effect, that there must be two *kinds* of truth: one accessible to theological and the other to scientific inquiry.

Yet such a distinction could not be maintained, since truth, whatever it is, must be one. A conflict between "science" and "religion" cannot be maintained permanently.

It was to such a tension between the "science" and the "religion" of the thirteenth century that Thomas Aquinas and other medieval schoolmen particularly addressed themselves, and they resolved it in terms of their own day. But as modern scientific procedures developed from the seventeenth century onwards, the tension reappeared in a more acute form. With the discovery of biological evolution resulting from the researches of Darwin, Wallace, and others in the nineteenth century, and the ensuing discovery of an even more fundamental evolutionary principle in all things, the conflict seemed at first to break out with renewed force. By the turn of the present century, however, the force of the battle was seen to be largely spent and among educated people it no longer seemed important. In the religious domain the evolutionary nature of the universe was gradually accepted and explained as "God's way of doing things," while in the scientific realm quantum physics and other developments that banished the old mechanistic conceptions of the universe made the most creative minds more open to philosophical and theological speculation.

I am satisfied that Unificationism is totally right in insisting that "The day must come when religion and science advance in one united way." (*Divine Principle*, p.4)

The task of the scientist is to uncover nature so that the human mind can grasp more and more of its workings. "Science," however, examines and can examine only one dimension of reality: the dimension we call "nature." The religious consciousness is concerned with the other dimension that we call "God": a spiritual dimension.

The question then must be: how are these two dimensions related? Why should both be accounted radically important? Why can neither assume superiority over the other? To this fundamental question we must return in a later section when we discuss the nature of God.

What has been said must not lead us to suppose that "science" and "religion" can now be easily blended together in an instant mix. But they must work together like two halves of the same scissors, each of which, when separated, has only a very limited use. Only together can they do the task for which they are intended. Except for mathematics, science and religion may be said to operate in ways more like each other than people commonly suppose. For unlike mathematics, which is of course a grand-scale tautology although an extremely valuable and indeed indispensable tautology, the sciences proceed by hypothesis and verification. It is a long and arduous process, with perhaps thousands of failures for every success. The religious man, the man of faith, proceeds likewise by experimentation. His mode of verification may seem even more arduous and certainly slower, for he must *live* the life of faith in order to make it his own in such a way that it yields knowledge of the spiritual world, knowledge of God. Yet all along he is realizing, be it ever so slowly, the Kingdom of God within his own life, so enhancing his confidence and sense of assurance even before he can call his faith full knowledge. This is an aspect of faith that has been much overlooked even in Reformation theology where faith is so much stressed. Calvin, however, shows clearly in the *Institutes* that faith produces a *kind* of cognition, yielding the blessed assurance of the saints. Moreover, as divine revelation comes to us as a joyous surprise, so also do the discoveries of science surprise us. Who could have expected the magnitude of the universe that we now know? In no way could one ever *deduce*, if one had never seen an oak tree, that it must exist, let alone that its leaves should have the shape they do have. The facts about the empirical world, as we discover them, are just as surprising in their own way as are the facts about the spiritual dimension of being. So despite the patently great difference in the methodology of the sciences on the one hand and that of philosophical theology on the other, there is a basis for much greater mutual understanding than is widely supposed. Never has this been clearer than with the advent of modern quantum physics and other scientific discoveries within the past hundred years.

God and Nature

Unificationist thought, inheriting much at this point from its great Chinese ancestry, recognizes a duality at the core of all things: the *yang* and the *yin*, the positive and the negative, which are sometimes said together to constitute the Tao. *Divine Principle* (I,1,2) suggests a parallel between the *yang-yin* as the creative principle issuing from *Taeguk* (the ultimate principle) and the Logos, the eternal principle in God that John, in his prologue, identifies with Jesus Christ, its manifestation in human flesh.

Divine Principle also, however (I,1,1)

adopts the concept that Plato used in his Timaeus when he portrayed God as an artist. "Just as we can sense an author's character through his works, so we can perceive God's deity by observing His creation." The work of creation is, then, an external manifestation of God's internal nature. That is implied in the Genesis story in which God, as he surveys each stage of his creation, pronounces it good; that is, it reflects his own goodness.

The notion of duality eternally springing from the unity of God is one that should be taken very seriously in the enunciation of the kind of philosophical expression of Unificationism that one would seek. A crucial question remains, however, in light of what has been already said about the concept of creation. If as the psalmist proclaims, "the heavens declare the glory of God and the firmament showeth His handiwork," we must ask why this is so. If we say that it is because it merely reflects the divine nature as my paintings of a sunset reflects the way in which my mind perceives sunsets, we run into various difficulties. Shakespeare at some point constructed *Hamlet* and at some other point constructed *Macbeth* (both, we might say, largely "out of his head") and no doubt it is true that there may have been something of Hamlet and something of Macbeth in his mind. Yet that is hardly what we mean, surely, and certainly not what Plato could have meant, by saying that the universe stands to God as the work of an artist to the artist himself.

Might we not say, however, that the reason the heavens declare the glory of God is that they are an aspect (though by no means the whole) of the Divine Nature? When we look at the "laws" of nature we are looking at an aspect of God, as the moral law expressed in the Torah or in karma-yoga, for instance, is an aspect of God. Nature is God as manifested in the working out of his activity, which as we have seen is fundamentally and eternally creative. Yet it is no more God than the thoughts I have are the mind that has them. It is the way in which God manifests himself and the law through which he works in creating all things. Yet it is not merely an artistic creation; it is an aspect of God as my thoughts are an aspect of me, not merely something I externalize on paper or canvas or on a piano or violin.

The laws of nature are God's laws, to be obeyed as we would obey God. In the spiritual dimension we are privileged to behold a more interior aspect of God's nature that transcends yet in no way contravenes the aspect made accessible to us in the empirical world. I would suggest that a view such as this could be and should be incorporated into Unificationist philosophy. It would in no radical way run counter to the teachings expressed in the *Divine Principle*.

The Mind and Heart of God

God is to be understood as "the Creator of all things" and therefore, as we have seen, eternally creating. He is "the absolute reality, eternally self-existent, transcendent of time and space." He is the source of all things.

As the source of all being he must encompass within himself, for example, intelligence superior to any intelligence we find manifested in His creation. In so far as personality is a value (as we suppose it to be), God must be personal *par excellence;* yet in so far as impersonality is to be accounted a value he is also impersonal *par excellence*.

According to the testimony of the Bible and much other religious literature, God is above all else loving. No sparrow, even, falls to the ground without His knowing of and caring about it. That is to say, God does not merely create and supervise and sustain his ongoing creative activity; He cares about it in the minutest detail. Using a human analogy we may say, therefore, that his heart beats for ever in love with his creation, not merely in a generalized and abstract way but for every one of his creatures as if it were the only one.[2] His heart goes out in a special and unique way to him who sighs in simple, humble longing for God. Such a poor man or woman is infinitely more important in his sight than a whole army of organized trumpeters professing to sing his praise. So, in Kierkegaard's terms God is "pure subjectivity"; He is not merely the object of creaturely adoration but the Eternal Subject confronting each individual soul.

Such a God is not what Pascal called "the God of the philosophers and scholars"; He is the living God, eternally acting on each one of his creatures, eternally available, eternally dependable. He is the eternal Other. Yet he is no less eternally permeating his creation and indeed suffering with it. The religions of the West (Judaism, Christianity, and Islam) have generally insisted on the otherness of God and his transcendence of his creation, while the great Eastern religions (Hinduism, Buddhism, for example) have tended to emphasize his immanence in creation. God, however, is more than can be encompassed by any of our straitjackets. In both the Western and the Eastern vision of God there is profound and most important truth; yet neither exhausts the mystery of divine Being. Our vision of God is always ludicrously too small.

So in God lie all the polarities we perceive in the universe, all the dualities, all the quaternities, all the trinities, yet he is above all the Eternal One. So also he is rightly said to be everywhere yet nowhere, both the Hegelian Absolute *Geist* and Dante's *l'amor che muove il sole e l'altre stelle.*

Restoration and the Ideal of God

Unificationism recognizes the power of evil in the universe. It entered into the scheme of things through the "serpent," symbolizing the angel (call him what you will) who "fell," that is, the angel who exercised his will in a way contrary to the will of God. So it is that "we wrestle not against flesh and blood, but against principalities, against powers, against the rulers of the darkness of this world, against spiritual wickedness in high places." (Eph. 6:12) Evil cannot inhere in God, but it can and does enter the created order through the exercise of freedom. Freedom of choice is a necessary endowment for creatures, since without it they could not choose right over wrong, God over the enemies of God. Creatures cannot make a real choice in favor of God unless they are also free to make such a choice against him. So freedom of choice is part of the scenario of creation. And spiritual and physical falls are always possible. Nevertheless, with the final triumph of the forces of good over the forces of evil, the redeemed will instinctively always choose the good, because they will have attained the clarity of vision that will preclude wrong choices.

Unification theology clearly envisions that humankind will one day realize the perfect unity in the love of God for which he is intended. In that process of "restoration," man will realize three blessings. The first is his ability to enter into and become aware of his own spirituality; the second is his ability to create a family and from that family, as the instrument of God's dominion of love, to unify the world as one family in that dominion of love; and the third is his ability to exercise spiritual and physical dominion over creation by the use of scientific and technological learning and skill.

Male and female sexuality have their roots, as has everything else, in God. They are intended not merely for the procreation and nurture of children and the propagation of the human race but for the full blooming of the spiritual nature of men and women. The family, although an instrument of God's love, is more than an instrument; it is its manifestation on earth and therefore sacramental in the fullest possible sense. Because the family is holy beyond all else in human institutions, sins against the family, such as adultery, are the most grievous of sins a human being can commit. (On this view the early Christians were right in classifying it with murder as among the sins which, when committed by a baptized Christian, entailed his or her expulsion from the Christian fellowship for ever.) Family love not only reflects but participates in the very Heart of God.

In a perfect world, therefore, we should find one vast family united in the Divine love. Distinctions of race, nationality, and religion would have disappeared. They would have become as meaningless to humanity as the distinctions between members of now extinct societies in the world of antiquity are to us today, having lost all political, cultural, and spiritual significance. God's love would rule His creation through the human family and its extension throughout the world.

The attainment of this ideal is precisely what is to be achieved through what is traditionally called "the Second Coming" and the triumph of good over evil, the fulfillment of the restorative process and the end of history as we understand it.

Notes

1. For further historical details of this kind see William N. Blair, *The Korean Pentecost* (New York: The Northern Presbyterian Board, 1908) and Chong H. Pyen, *Han Kuk Ku Tok Kyo Sa,* History of the Korean Christian Church, (Seoul: Shim Woo Won Press, 1959); also Elizabeth Younghee Kwon, *A Study of the Growth of the Presbyterian Church in Korea:* a thesis for the degree of Master of Arts in the University of Southern California, 1962, which, as chairman of her committee, I directed.

2. I have expounded my view of God as suffering and as in travail in, with, and through his creation, in *He Who Lets Us Be: A Theology of Love* (New York: Seabury Press, 1975), reprinted with a revised preface (New York: Paragon House Publishers, 1987).

The Unification
of World and Spirit
in the Thought
of Reverend
Sun Myung Moon

Joseph Bettis

Ladies and Gentlemen, distinguished guests: In some ways it is a curious circumstance that I, a Westerner, from a country as new as the United States, should have the honor of speaking to you about Reverend Sun Myung Moon, a man shaped and molded by the ancient traditions of the East. Please permit me, therefore, simply to share with you some of my thoughts about the significance of Reverend Moon and his thought from the perspective of his impact on the society and culture of the West.

I have known Reverend Moon for nine years. During that time I have come to realize that he is a man of cosmic inspiration. He is a man of great spirituality, with a magnificent vision of what our world might be. He is also a man of great personal warmth and love. He loves his family deeply, he loves all human beings, and he loves his God. He is a man of humor and wit, capable of bringing tears of happiness to many people. It is a great honor for me to be able to speak to you briefly about him.

I shall not present a systematic exposition of Reverend Moon's thought. I am not competent to do so, nor does it seem to me that such an approach is appropriate in this situation. Rather I wish to pick three subjects that seem to me to be both central to his understanding and also especially important in the context of his impact on the West. These three items are: (1) religious pluralism, (2) politics, and (3) the family.

Religious Pluralism

Our world is becoming increasingly divided between *sectarianism* and *secularism*. Sectarianism is religious provincialism; it is the belief that one's own religious tradition is the only true path.

Dr. Joseph Bettis
on the speaking tour

Secularism, on the other hand, is the belief that none of the religious traditions are valid. What our world needs is a way between sectarianism and secularism. This third way, or middle path, is *religious pluralism:* the recognition of the value of many different religious traditions.

I am aware that religious pluralism is more familiar in the East than in the West. It is common in the West for religious practice to be associated with a particular idea of truth. According to this understanding, truth is embodied in ideas, and any idea that is different is untrue. In other words, *difference* is a mark of untruth and should, therefore, be stamped out. This is a sectarian idea of truth. So the history of the West has been dominated by religious struggle and war, characterized by the attempt to convert other people to one's own religious beliefs and practices. This motivation has dominated, and continues to characterize, most of the conflict in the West, between the major power blocs as well as between Christians and Muslims.

The alternative to sectarian fragmentation and division has taken the form of technological secularism. Free of sectarian bias, secular society is able to establish economic and political communication across wide geographic areas. Cooperation has been achieved through ignoring religious and cultural traditions. The results, however, have been devastating. In addition to the mindless rush toward nuclear holocaust and environmental destruction, the West has created conditions throughout the world in which culture after culture is faced with the dilemma of choosing either modernization with the loss of tradition, or tradition at the expense of modernization. Secularism, as an alternative to sectarianism, has demonstrated that it will not work.

As an alternative to sectarianism or secularism, Reverend Moon has advanced the concept of *Unification:* cultural harmony built on the recognition of the importance of cultural diversity and religious pluralism. In many ways, for example, through the creation of the New Ecumenical Research Association, Reverend Moon has brought together religious leaders and thinkers from every religious tradition in ways that have enabled them to experience first hand the advantages and strengths of a vital pluralism.

Reverend Moon has taught us that we have nothing to fear from diversity. On the contrary, religious diversity encourages and adds vitality and life to our common human enterprise. Just as a vase of flowers is more interesting and beautiful because it contains flowers of different colors and kinds, our human community is more lively and vital if it includes a variety of religious and cultural expressions. Each of us is just one individual. Our own experience is limited by time and space. But together we are many human beings with a wide and diverse set of experiences. Our own limited humanity is expanded by others, therefore, and to the degree that we can share our different experiences our humanity is more nearly complete.

Politics beyond Idealism and Materialism

In the political arena, Reverend Moon's vision is of a political world beyond both idealism and materialism.

While there are many forces at work in our modern world striving to bring us together in peace and harmony, there are also forces seeking to pull us

apart and destroy us. This conflict between the forces of light and darkness is a struggle that is as old as the world. At present its most dramatic manifestation takes the form of the struggle between atheistic materialism and religious idealism.

In this struggle, the thought of Reverend Moon takes a complex and at times apparently contradictory course. On one hand, Reverend Moon considers atheistic communism to be the greatest single threat to the future of the human race. His opposition to communism began years ago during the time of the conflict in Korea, and continues unabated into the present.

At the same time, Reverend Moon also recognizes that past forms of Western idealism are inadequate. He is no more favorably disposed toward anti-religious capitalism than he is toward atheistic communism. This has led Reverend Moon to advance a new vision for the political-social world, a vision that moves beyond capitalism and communism, toward a world in which the practical affairs of human beings, in their political and economic lives, are infused by a religious spirit of universal love, compassion and cooperation.

In his ability to combine strong opposition to communism with a recognition that the ultimate objective is the transcendence of the contemporary ideological conflict, Reverend Moon has envisioned a new political direction, beyond the confines of previous alternatives.

The Family

Central to both Reverend Moon's religious and political vision is his concept of family.

It is fairly common to recognize that

alienation is the dominant characteristic of advanced technological civilizations. Alienation has not been limited to the West. As country after country throughout the world has moved from pre-industrialization to high technology, the loss of tradition and social stability has been accompanied by a predictable increase in personal and collective alienation. Relationships between human beings, at the personal, family, national and international levels, have become increasingly strained and stressed as this process has evolved.

Neither the collectivism in some countries nor the individualism of others has proved an adequate response. What is needed is a new conceptualization of the fabric of human community and the interdependence of the individual and the group. Reverend Moon's emphasis on the family as the center of religious and political life provides just such a new conceptualization. The family, according to Reverend Moon, is neither the anti-social and reactionary structure that Marx thought it was; nor is the conventional nuclear or ancestral family the repository of all social stability as conservatives claim. On the contrary, Reverend Moon sees the emerging family as a dynamic structure, centered in the love of God and encompassing the love of husband and wife, and of parents for children, in a way that provides both stable structure and energetic growth for individuals and societies.

This emphasis on the family as the basis for the post modern community, beyond alienation, constitutes a singular and vital alternative to collectivism on one hand and individualism on the other.

Conclusion

In conclusion, I want to turn from the thought to the thinker. The impact that Reverend Moon has made on the West has been not only through his thought, but also through the power of his personal presence. Those of you who have had the privilege of meeting him or hearing him speak can testify to this. He is a man of immense energy and will, and this energy expresses itself in a way that can only be experienced.

Reverend Moon is not content, however, to rely on his personal charisma. He continually translates his personal energy into social projects. Reverend Moon has created literally dozens of organizations, institutions, and projects dedicated to making our world a better place for all human beings. I am personally familiar with several of them. Significantly, they are not designed only for members of the Unification Church, or to promote the doctrines of Reverend Moon. These organizations are open to all people of good faith—of any religious persuasion or of none—who are dedicated to the ideals of a better world. I am not a member of Reverend Moon's church, although I am privileged to participate in these projects and to share in his vision for a better world. I know of no other religious leader who is more eager for people of all persuasions to share in a common effort.

My point is this, and here I end. There is no other living religious leader, East or West, who has done more in the contemporary world, to envision a new reality beyond the present political and religious dilemmas; no other religious leader who has done more to bring East and West together; no other religious leader who has worked harder to build real organizations and institutions for social change; and no other religious leader who has devoted more divinely inspired energy to the pursuit of worldwide peace and harmony. I am deeply grateful for the opportunities I have had to learn from Reverend Moon, and to share with you something of my opinion about the significance of his life and thought for the future of our shared humanity.

Thank you.

TWO

ECUMENICAL AND INTERFAITH ACTIVITIES

The Interreligious Future:
The Contributions and Implications of the Thought and Work of the Reverend Sun Myung Moon

M. Darrol Bryant

I consider it a great honor to have been invited to address you concerning the Reverend Sun Myung Moon, your fellow countryman and one of the great religious leaders of our time. It has been my privilege since 1977 to have been associated with several of Reverend Moon's initiatives in the United States in relation to the task of interreligious dialogue. From the founding of the Unification Theological Seminary to the establishment of the New Ecumenical Research Association (New ERA), through the beginning of the Council for the World's Religions (CWR), to the recent Assembly of World Religions, Reverend Moon has consistently championed the cause of interreligious dialogue and cooperation. And I am grateful for this opportunity to share with you something of that great work.

I apologize for my inability to address you in your own language and beg your indulgence for addressing you in English.

I

As you are all painfully aware, our world is broken by many divisions. We are daily assailed by news of conflict between East and West, North and South, rich and poor, between generations and between religious communities. Indeed, some have called ours a century of war and revolution, something you here on the Korean peninsula have painfully experienced. It is certainly true to say that we have been caught up in a great transformation that is altering the face of our common planet. The winds of change are everywhere. These are times when it is easy to despair and lose hope, times when we become disoriented. And it is precisely in the midst of such disjointed

M. Darroll Bryant

times and painful events that Korea has given to the world a champion of vision, unity and hope: the Reverend Sun Myung Moon. In the very midst of turmoil he has heeded a Divine Calling to bear witness to a higher purpose: the unity of the whole human family in relation to God. This purpose is rooted, Reverend Moon believes, in the very heart of God. It is a purpose as old as creation itself yet ever in need of new articulations, a purpose that requires new champions, a purpose that demands our best efforts.

Traditionally people have found the answers to the most fundamental questions of life in their religious faith. It is faith that connects us to the deeper purposes of the whole cosmos. But the whirl of change that we have endured in our century has also affected our religious traditions. Too often our religious traditions have become too narrow; rather than opening us out to the larger purposes of God, they have become the bastions of exlusivity. We are in need, then, of a truly global spirituality that is adequate to our emergent situation. We need a global spirituality that will orient us anew amidst the challenges and conflicts of our time. Central to the quest for a new global spirituality is the necessity for a fruitful dialogue between the religions of the world, one that will allow them to be mutually transformed in relation to their Divine Source. It is here that I believe Reverend Moon is making his most lasting and significant contribution, one that will bear fruits over the coming decades and that may well lead to a truly global spirituality. Let me share with you some of those beginnings.

II

In 1977 I attended the first "theologians conference" held at the Unification Theological Seminary in Barrytown, New York. This conference was held to bring theologians from different Christian denominations into conversation with the Unification movement. Over four days of spirited exchange, we explored various aspects of the teaching of the Unification movement with students at the Seminary. What began to emerge in these conversations were two things. First, that we could all be enlarged and grow through dialogue and exchange with one another. And, secondly, that in the Unification movement was a spirit and vision that required us all to think in more global terms. We could not be content with just reiterating the teachings of our particular denominations, but we were all challenged to move toward a more inclusive vision of the whole human family. For many of us this was our first encounter with a religious movement that took seriously and incorporated into itself the wisdom of the East. Rather than looking disparagingly at the East, the Unification movement had incorporated into itself a vision that transcended the conventional dichotomies of East and West.

Over the next couple of years these conversations continued and the circle of people drawn into them became wider. We then began to realize that we were involved in a conversation that included not only the whole spectrum of Christian denominations, but persons in other traditions as well. Out of these beginnings there emerged in 1980 the New Ecumenical Research Association (New ERA). This new ecumenical venture included not only Christian thinkers but also people from Buddhist, Hindu, Islamic, and Confucian traditions. We were on our way to becoming an association that was truly ecumenical in the root meaning of that term: *the whole inhabited earth.* As was said in the founding documents of New ERA, we sought to build a global conversation based on the vision of the *family of religious traditions.* We sought to take seriously the multiform religious heritage of humankind, one that included the wisdom of the East as well as the West, of the South as well as the North.

As New ERA took off, we sponsored as many as thirty conferences in a given year that explored a range of issues that cut across the many religious traditions. In 1981 we held the first of what I consider the most important achievement of New ERA: the conference on "God: The Contemporary Discussion." Here we held what was truly one of the most remarkable events in the religious history of humankind. Rather than a gathering of just Christian, or just Islamic, or just Buddhist, or just Hindu, or just Confucian scholars, theologians, and religious leaders, we sought to bring people from all these traditions together in relation to the most basic question of all: the question of God, the Ultimate. At this first conference in Hawaii over 180 scholars from around the world, and from virtually every tradition, met to probe the contemporary meaning of our varied beliefs about, and faith in the Transcendent. It was a truly historic occasion. Few if any such meetings have ever been held. And here we had persons from all the traditions trying to explain to one another in an atmosphere of mutual respect their deepest convictions concerning the Divine Ground of all life.

These conferences have continued; the fourth such conference was held in Seoul in August 1984. Out of these conferences have emerged a series of volumes. The first, edited by Professor Frederick Sontag and myself, was simply entitled *God: The Contemporary Discussion;* and one reviewer called it a "landmark volume towards the development of a world theology." Seven other volumes have now appeared that deal with topics ranging from "Spiritual Discipline and Ultimate Reality" to "Women in the Great Traditions" to "God and Global Justice." All of this work is contributing to a truly global dialogue involving persons in all traditions. No longer will it be possible for the religious traditions to exist in ignorance of one another, or with hostility towards one another. Increasingly, all of us have to discover ourselves and the Ultimate anew amidst the global dialogue of religions.

New ERA also contributed to other disciplines through its annual conference on the Sociology of Religion. Here too top scholars from around the world were brought together to consider major issues in the sociology of religion. The first such conference in 1981 led to a volume on the *Social Impact of New Religious Movements* edited by Professor Bryan Wilson of Oxford University. In subsequent years a distinguished series of volumes has emerged edited by leading scholars in the field of the sociology of religion. Over the years New ERA has sponsored numerous other conferences as well.

Through New ERA, then, an international association of scholars has been created that is contributing to the search for a global spirituality adequate to the demands of our age. While membership in the Unification movement is not a prerequisite for participation in this association, it must be acknowledged that the movement has contributed both the financial and spiritual resources—as well as the dedicated personnel—that have made it possible. Moreover it has been the contribution of Reverend Moon to have challenged scholars to risk a new form of community and collaboration beyond the divisions of discipline and religious tradition that far too often characterize the academic world. As ranking scholars within varied traditions and from various disciplines encounter one another in a spirit of goodness and respect for one another, they are charting a way ahead that can contribute to a truly new era.

III

A second initiative in the area of inter-religious dialogue is the Council for the World's Religions which had its first meeting in the Fall of 1984. Building on the foundation of New ERA, the CWR has sought to build bridges of understanding and to promote unity both within religious traditions and between traditions. Its aim has been both intra-religious dialogue and inter-religious dialogue. Moreover, it has sought to include religious leaders as well as scholars in its work. Over the past two years it has convened a series of intrareligious conferences that have brought together persons from the different strands of the Jewish, Islamic, Buddhist, Christian, and Hindu traditions. In each of these meetings the participants have explored the sources of conflict within their respective traditions and sought ways of promoting intrareligious unity and harmony.

Following the New ERA pattern, the

CWR has brought together a distinguished Board of Consultants from the different religious traditions to plan and carry out its activities. While New ERA was more heavily centered in the Christian traditions, the CWR has from the outset been more focused across the range of traditions. On its Board are to be found Hindus and Moslems, Buddhists and Jews, Christians and a representative of a primal African religion. Unlike other interfaith organizations, the CWR conceives of itself as serving the several traditions in relation to their own ultimate grounds and purposes.

This is a brave initiative. Despite the suggestion of critics that such projects serve merely to enhance the reputation of the Unification movement, the record of the Council makes clear that its purpose is to serve one of the great imperatives of our age: spiritual unity and cooperation between traditions.

In a world such as ours, broken by religious, ideological, political and social conflict, it is increasingly imperative that we attain a new vision of the spiritual unity of the human race that will undergird cooperation in other spheres of life. Only as we come to see and understand ourselves in relation to our Divine Parent will we gain the will to secure unity throughout the human family. Such a vision does not require uniformity because a family is enhanced by its very diversity and multiformity. We grow and are enriched by the variety of gifts present in a family and at the same time we are united in relation to our transcendent Source. Too often in our materialistic age we neglect to recognize the spiritual nature of human beings. It is precisely the aim of the CWR to recover and promote the spiritual unity of the human family.

Again, this was an initiative that required vision, daring and courage. While many in our century have spoken of the need for a truly interreligious dialogue, few religious leaders have actually moved in this direction. Far too often religious leaders are preoccupied with the need to build their own faith community and its institutions. But the uniqueness of Reverend Moon is that he has attempted to build what the American theologian Harvey Cox has called "metainstitutions." A metainstitution incorporates into itself differences which normal institutions consider a threat. Thus rather than serving the interests of a particular group, a metainstitution seeks to serve a higher purpose that will, in the course of its life, transform all the participants in ways that as yet cannot be anticipated. Rather than simply being a Christian or a Buddhist or a Hindu etcetera institution, the CWR seeks to be a metainstitution serving the purposes of God in relation to the different religious traditions.

Over the coming years it is quite possible that the CWR will emerge as the leading forum for inter- and intra-religious dialogue and alliance. As both scholars and religious leaders cooperate in the work of CWR, a new history of interreligious cooperation, respect and harmony is in the process of being born. And it is the God-centered vision of Reverend Moon that has made it possible.

IV

A third major initiative launched by Reverend Moon is the Assembly of the World's Religions. The first of these meetings was held near New York City in November of 1985. Here more than

600 participants and another 300 family members and staff—nearly 1000 people—from more than 80 countries and from every major and virtually every minor religious tradition participated. Here we gathered a truly representative microcosm of the whole family of religious traditions on our planet. From the East and West, North and South, young and old, Buddhist, Jew, Sikh, Hindu, Christian, Moslem, Taoist, Confucianist, African primal religions and new religious movements, they all came for a truly remarkable week of interreligious exchange. As one of the participant remarked at the end of the Assembly: "I felt like hope was born anew in this Assembly. Who would have believed that people with such diverse backgrounds and different religious commitments could have experienced the kind of spiritual unity we experienced here? It was thrilling. I go home with a new vision of what is possible for humankind."

An event of such magnitude is impossible to adequately describe here. But you may be interested to know the following: First, the entire Assembly was planned by a committee involving persons from all the major religious traditions. And, rather than seeking a "lowest common denominator" approach, we were all convinced that the Assembly would truly work only if we came together out of the depths of our respective traditions. Thus the participants were encouraged to write and speak out their most deeply held experiences of Divine life as that was known to them in their own traditions. Secondly, each day began with prayer and meditation by tradition, but open to participants from other traditions who wanted to pray or meditate in the Mos-

lem or Hindu or Christian or Buddhist or Jewish or Sikh or Confucianist way. These daily prayer and meditation sessions provided the spiritual foundation for each day. Thirdly, each day included three to four hours of small group sessions involving not more than twenty people in a group on one or another of the Assembly's thirteen themes. In these groups people shared their spiritual journeys as well as their reflections on the topics that ranged from "family life and learning" to "spiritual disciplines" to "poverty and human rights." In all of these groups a spirit of sharing developed that was truly transformative to the participants. As one of them remarked: "I was truly changed by coming into contact with people from traditions and cultures I had never before known. I discovered both differences and remarkable points of similarity. I was challenged, sometimes upset, but I truly grew to love and appreciate everyone in my group. Wouldn't it be wonderful if this were happening all over the planet!" These small groups constituted the heart of each day—and the center of the Assembly experience for the individual participants.

This Assembly succeeded beyond our highest expectations. It gave substance to the hope and dream that people of different religious traditions might collaborate and contribute to the common future of humankind, that differences can enrich and be the occasion for growth in our understanding of the Transcendent and our life together on this planet. These Assemblies will continue into the future with meetings planned for 1989 and 1993, the 100th Anniversary of the great Parliament of the World's Religions in Chicago in 1893.

In these events a new day is dawning in the religious life of the human race, one that will have profound and lasting consequences in humanity's quest for fulness and unity in relation to God.

V

The projects which I have described above are, of course, but one aspect of Reverend Sun Myung Moon's work in America for the sake of the whole world. None of these projects would have been possible without his vision and generosity. Indeed, they are intimately related to and grow out of three aspects of Reverend Moon's teaching that should be noted here.

First, there is the vision of the unity of humankind in relation to God that is central to the teaching of Reverend Moon. This vision of unity is not uniformity, but incorporates into itself diversity as complimentarity. Thus in Reverend Moon's vision of unity, differences are to be orchestrated into a complex whole, with each religious tradition discovering itself in relation to the other traditions and in relation to the Divine Ground and Purpose in the building up of our common life. Such a vision is what is most desperately required to move us beyond the impasses of the present. And it is precisely Reverend Moon's vocation to bear witness to this Divine Imperative.

Secondly, there is the "give and take" principle of Reverend Moon's teaching. This aspect is crucial because it means that the way towards our unity is out of a process of dialogue and exchange, of give and take. This cosmic principle of Divine life is also central to the relations

between traditions. As you can see from the projects described above, there is no attempt to impose a false or artificial or ideological uniformity on the relation between traditions. Rather, the commitment is to dialogue and exchange as the *way*, the process that must be undergone and endured, so that unity can emerge. It is out of give and take, giving and receiving, listening and speaking, that we will find our way to that unity that can truly enhance us all.

And thirdly, there is the principle that our spiritual commitments should issue in practical benefits to humankind. In Reverend Moon's teaching we see a commitment to a unity of theory and practice, of vision and social improvement. This has important consequences for our work as well in that it keeps us from endless speculation and insists that we bend our efforts in ways that will overcome the great problems that face us all in the practical order. In Reverend Moon's terms, we must work to overcome the suffering heart of God, and that suffering is transformed when we build fruitful relations within ourselves, among persons and groups, between traditions and cultures, between races and peoples. In this way, then, we contribute simultaneously to binding up the broken heart of God and a broken human family.

It is my hope that you will join the Reverend Sun Myung Moon in this great work. He has given us a vision and a direction and has dedicated his life to the achievement of this vision. I have personally gained tremendously through my association with Reverend Moon and his work and I believe he has initiated a work that is pleasing to God and for the benefit of humankind.

An Ecumenical Faith: Reverend Moon and the Unification Church

Frank K. Flinn

It is my honor to be able to speak before you as a Roman Catholic theologian. I am going to begin my story in a personal way. In 1976 I was completing my doctoral studies in religion at the University of St. Michael's College at the Toronto School of Theology. One day I was walking down the corridor at the university and passed Professor Herbert Richardson. I said "Hello!" and passed him by. Professor Richardson then called out and tossed me a book, saying "Flinn, why don't you read this book and tell me what you think of it." The book was *Divine Principle*.

I took the book home and set it on my desk, where it lay for about a month. One evening, looking for something different to read, I opened the book and read it cover to cover in one sitting. The book fascinated me in many ways. While it is not a sophisticated theological treatise, it does contain some vitally important theological insights about Creation and Restoration. Likewise I noted that *Divine Principle* is unique in a special way: at the very center of its theological concern *Divine Principle* is ecumenical. Most of the religions of the western world begin with a principle of exclusiveness. One claims to have the unique Law of God, another claims the sole Savior, and another upholds the last Prophet. When these religions come to reach true ecumenical dialogue, they still do so with the presupposition that "My way is the only way." I sensed that *Divine Principle* was saying "The only way is through our many ways" for bringing about the Kingdom of God on earth. At the heart of Unification theology is the acceptance of the religion of others. It is not exclusive but inclusive in its theological foundation. Perhaps that is why Unification

Theology places so much emphasis on the theological meaning of "heart." The "heart" is the organ by which we accept others.

Shortly after reading *Divine Principle* I ran across a report by the Faith and Order Commission of the National Council of Churches in the United States. This report attacked *Divine Principle* for its interpretation of the Bible. At the same time, Professor Richardson was organizing a small conference on the Unification Movement at the Toronto School of Theology. He asked me to write a paper on how *Divine Principle* interpreted the Bible. In that paper, and many subsequent essays, I have tried to show that *Divine Principle's* interpretation of the Bible is much like the interpretation of the Bible in the Middle Ages in Europe, and has been strongly influenced by the dispensational understanding of God's plan in history as found in the widely used Scoffield Bible. This dispensational reading of the Bible, I might add, was strongly present in Puritan theology and shaped the vision of the Protestant Christian missionaries who came to Korea, China and Japan in the late 19th century.

Sometime after the Toronto Conference on Unification Theology I was invited down to the Unification Theological Seminary in Barrytown, New York. I must admit that I went with some fear and trepidation. I had read some newspaper articles which did not treat Reverend Moon and the Unification Church very kindly. My experience at the Seminary was wonderful, most of all because the students were genuinely shaped by the ecumenical vision in *Divine Principle*. The Principle is not just

Japanese shrine drawn by Dr. Frank Flinn

a book but a way of life for people of faith.

Over the course of the next few years I became deeply involved in ecumenical dialogues both at the Unification Theological Seminary and elsewhere. In 1980 Reverend Moon assembled a group of theologians of all faiths and invited them to pursue ecumenical interchange on a worldwide basis. This group was founded as New ERA (the New Ecumenical Research Association). New ERA today continues as one of the many aspects of the IRF (International Religious Foundation), which has brought forth manifold fruits in a worldwide Garden of Ecumenism.

I would like to conclude with a meditation on ecumenism and how my thoughts about ecumenism have been changed by my exposure to *Divine Principle* and Unification Theology. First, Reverend Moon in *Divine Principle* states that the primary image of God for our time is as Divine Parent. If God is our Parent, then all of us are related. On the surface we see differences in races, tribes, and nations. But spiritually we are brothers and sisters. Secondly, because we are all related and we all bear the image of our True Parent, Unification Theology is a theology of relations. In *Divine Principle* this is called "give-and-take."

Thirdly, because all of us are called to "give-and-take" action in order to restore the original purpose of Creation in all levels of life, each religion is called to let other religions to be both givers and takers. No one can claim a copyright on the Truth. This means, in a way, that all of us are asked to have more than one faith if all the faiths of the world are to find their common ecu-

Dr. Flinn's letter to Rev. Moon

menical heart. I am called to bear the faith of others in my veins and bones.

In the Old Testament, the prophet Amos challenged Israel to recognize that the Lord of History is Lord of all peoples. The ancient Israelites tended to think that they were special because the Lord gave them the Exodus and brought them out of bondage in Egypt. But Amos proclaimed that God gave even foreign nations their Passovers:

> The Lord said:
> O children of Israel,
> Did I not bring up Israel out of the land of Egypt?
> And the Philistines from Caphtor?
> And the Syrians from Kir?
> (Amos 8:6)

In this passage from the Bible the most important event in the life of a single people is made both concrete and universal. The Unification Movement wants to make that vision real for the whole earth by entering give and take action with all religions. Unificationism does not simply engage in dialogue; it *serves* dialogue.

Fourthly, Reverend Moon and the Unification Movement have vastly expanded the notion of ecumenism. What is needed in our time is not simply a dialogue between different religions, but also between theologians and economists, and philosophers and politicians, scientists and poets. This explains why the Unification Movement has expended so much time and energy on such projects as ICUS (International Conference on the Unity of the Sciences), ICF (International Cultural Foundation), and the IFVOC (International Federation for Victory Over Communism).

Here I would like to point out what the Unification opposition to Commu-nism is about. I think that Karl Marx began to see a truth when, in his early writings, he saw that the fundamental problem of economics had to do with "*relations* of production." But as atheistic communism unfolded in history and became Marxism-Leninism, the original ideal of right relations became distorted. There developed a mentality of oppression by others (a "poor me, I am a victim" attitude), a politics of resentment between classes, and a sociology of labelling those who disagree as "class enemies." If oppression, resentment, and labelling are our fundamental attitudes, how then can right relations be restored? Surely, no one wants to see oppressed peoples continue in their suffering, but so often liberation from a reign of oppressors simply paves the way for further oppression because the essence of true ecumenism cannot be established on the basis of resentment. This, I believe, is the reason for the opposition to current communist regimes. Unification offers, in place of politics of opposition and resentment, a theology of relations based on our fundamental relation to God as Parent. Unification wants to overcome the politics of resentment not with a gun but with heart. That is why conferees of all political persuasions are welcomed at the various dialogues. The important point, is that ecumenism can no longer remain regional; it must become universal if God's Kingdom is to grow and flourish.

Finally, I would like to share with you the feelings I had while attending the Assembly of World Religions, held at McAfee, in New Jersey, in November, 1985. This was the first of four international ecumenical gatherings held to continue the pioneering work of the

World Parliament of Religions, held in Chicago in 1893. All the major and many of the minor religions of the world were represented. Buddhists, Christians, Hindus, Muslims, Sikhs, American Indians, Shintoists, and many others conversed together, ate together, and worshipped together.

In his keynote address "Dialogue and alliance," Reverend Moon said:

> As far as I know, God is not sectarian. He is not obsessed with minor details of doctrine. We should quickly liberate ourselves from theological conflict which results from blind attachment to doctrines and rituals, and instead focus on living communication with God.

At this Assembly one could feel the pulse of the ecumenical heart of mankind beyond all differences of doctrine and worship. The Assembly was the most remarkable ecumenical and religious experience of my lifetime. One participant, Jocelyn Hellig of Johannesburg, South Africa, wrote afterward from her tension-torn nation:

> The Assembly was a living testimonial

to the fact that people of diverse cultures, religions and nationalities can not only live together harmoniously but they can, under the right conditions, come to know and understand one another as persons—and all conditions were right indeed.

The Unification Church is dedicated to serving the "right conditions" for the coming of God's ecumenical Kingdom on Earth. In response to the ecumenism of the Unification Church, Kenneth Cracknell of the British Council of Churches wrote in *Interfaith News* (February 1986):

> The Unification Church (which is not an orthodox Christian Church) does more for the interfaith movement at an international level than do either the World Council of Churches Dialogue unit or the Roman Catholic Vatican Secretariat for Non-Christians, or both of them put together.

I suggest that such an accomplishment stems from the fact that ecumenism lies within the heart of the Unification Movement and that its Founder has deeply experienced the reality that "God is not a sectarian."

The Interfaith Vision and Achievement of Reverend Sun Myung Moon and his Church

Francis Clark

When the dust of controversy settles and the smears of prejudice are wiped away by the hand of time, what will historians of the future see as most significant in the vision and work of Reverend Sun Myung Moon? No one can venture a confident prophecy to answer such a question. But looking at the question from the viewpoint of my own religious concerns and my lifelong interests, I would single out one field of his activity which I see as of the highest importance for the sake of our human family and its future. I refer to his world-embracing vision, and his already effective achievement, for bringing about global harmony between religions and universal fellowship among believers.

Reverend Moon proclaimed that vision in an address which he sent to the fourth international conference on "God: The Contemporary Discussion," which he convened in Seoul, in August 1984. His message was heard by the 250 delegates from all over the world, belonging to the main faiths of humankind. It was also heard by the 140 participants of the third Youth Seminar for World Religions, another of his interfaith projects, who were also present in Korea at the same time. Reverend Moon's address, delivered on that occasion, eloquently expresses the universal vision to which I have referred:

> As representatives of the world's religions you are called to bring your churches, mosques, synagogues, shrines and temples into a cooperative unity for the sake of world peace and human freedom, centered on God... Many people ask what religion can do in this secular age. I answer: the world's religions must provide a stable, universal foundation of values upon which governments can build true peace and harmony, science and

Dr. Francis Clark
in Tochigi, Japan

technology can be fully utilized for the happiness of mankind, and the world's cultures can be purified, exalted, shared and celebrated... Truly, the ideal I am espousing is nothing other than the Kingdom of God on Earth. I see it as a realistic goal toward which we can realistically work.

That vision, those words, speak directly to my own heart. I have long aspired towards the same ideals, and it is because Reverend Moon is putting those ideals into practical effect in a unique program which affects men and women in all continents that I am here today declaring my profound admiration for what he and his movement are doing for mankind in this vital area of human concern.

As well as proclaiming that great positive vision for inter-religious harmony as the blueprint of the future progress of the human race, Reverend Moon also reminds mankind that present wars, strife and enmity between peoples are embittered by religious factors. The outreach of believers in what is called "the wider ecumenism," embracing other believers and other religions in fraternal love and understanding, is therefore urgently necessary as a means to put out the fires of those enmities which imperil human co-existence in so many parts of the world. I quote again from his words at the God Conference of 1984:

I put the greatest emphasis on the ecumenical movement.... A major problem facing humanity today is the lack of spiritual unity among and within the world's religions. Despite all efforts to the contrary, divisions and animosities among various religious groups continue. Religious wars are still being waged, as they have been for centuries. In spite of various ecumenical movements, religious arrogance, intolerance and bigotry are still prevalent among devout believers. Thus, although most religions have professed the same God and often the same view for centuries, followers of those great religious traditions have continually persecuted and warred with one another... Yet as many great religious leaders have taught, because we are all children of the same Heavenly Parent we are all brothers and sisters in one great family, and inter-religious conflict and divisive hatred are unnecessary.

Again, I recognize in Reverend Moon's words and ideals my own deepest concerns. It is because I share those ideals, and because he, more than any one else, has taken an extraordinary initiative to make those ideals an effective reality, that I, a Catholic, thankfully respond to his call and collaborate in the world-wide program of practical projects which offers a real hope of fulfilling those ideals.

For the first time in human history it has become practically possible to promote a global dialogue between the diverse religions of the world, and to bring believers in all lands together in mutual respect, understanding and effective action for the welfare of mankind. The advance of science and technology, and the revolution in communications, have now made it possible for believers of all faiths to meet together to discuss the ultimates of human life and aspiration, and to bring to bear the universal force of religion to direct the future of our global family, under the guidance of God, our common Father.

This is no mere academic study, but a task of extreme urgency. The technological revolution has a more sinister aspect: there is a doom-laden threat to the well-being of all peoples, and even to the survival of life on our planet. The spectre of nuclear holocaust hangs over us. There is the terrible possibility that through failing to know, understand and love one another men will destroy human society.

Even if that ultimate catastrophe can be averted, there are still the massive pressures of the world's other intractable problems—problems of world hunger, of over-population, of disease, of failing world resources, of the threatened global environment. All that fosters understanding between the different nations and races, between faiths and ideologies, contributes towards lessening the danger of world destruction, and towards bringing about world peace, justice and community. Religion has a central place here. To establish the Kingdom of God among men is not just a dream, but a necessity. It is this realization that is the ruling motivation of Reverend Moon, and that governs all his work for inter-religious harmony.

I should like to describe briefly some of the important projects in this field which owe their existence and their dynamism to the initiative of Reverend Moon, and also to say something about my own association with those projects.

I have devoted myself to inter-religious outreach for many years. As Head of Religious Studies at the Open University, England, I conceived and directed a major program for the sympathetic study of human religion and religious ideals. It was a course entitled, "Man's Religious Quest," which has now been in progress for nearly ten years. During that time many thousands of students have followed the course, many as part of a degree program, others as non-graduating students following the course for professional advancement or personal interest. The textbooks which we wrote for the course, and the accompanying television films, radio presentations and other materials, have been widely used in many other countries as well as in Great Britain.

My experience in that program has brought me into contact with a wide cross-section of the population, and has shown me how lively is the interest in religious questions, and how profound is the religious instinct, even in those sectors of society which are not connected with institutional religions and which are usually thought of as secularized. I longed to be able to do something more effective, not merely in the academic sphere, but also in the real world of human life and action, to implement the inter-religious ideals which I felt so strongly. The opportunity has been presented to me through collaboration with the inter-religious projects of the Unification Church, initiated by Reverend Moon, and implemented mainly through The International Religious Foundation (IRF), which he founded as an overall organization to promote the specific projects.

One of the earliest interfaith projects promoted by IRF was New ERA—the New Ecumenical Research Association. This organization has promoted numerous conferences and other programs in America, Europe and elsewhere in order to foster understanding between believers. The participants were at first mainly from Christian backgrounds, but as the years went by people of other faiths became more and more involved.

Another boldly imaginative venture promoted by Reverend Moon through IRF is the Youth Seminar on World Religions. Each summer since 1982, a group of some 140 young people of many nations and faiths have been given the extraordinary opportunity of travelling around the world in order to study the faiths of others and to visit the holy places and homelands of the principal religions of the world. I myself have lectured to these young interfaith pilgrims each year when they visited Rome, in order to give them an account of the history and beliefs of Christianity, to conduct them to the historic sites, and to awaken in them a sense of their inter-religious fellowship. Other lecturers have taught them in Jerusalem, in Cairo, in Istanbul, in Benares, in Nepal, in Delhi, in Madras, in Bangkok, in China, in Korea, in the United States and other places.

The results of the Youth Seminar on World Religions have been profound, both for individuals and collectively. The young participants return from their world-wide interfaith pilgrimage strengthened in their grasp of their own faith, but now imbued with a new reverence and understanding for the faiths of others and a resolve to further the ideals of international religious fellowship. I know of no other interfaith educational program which can compare, both in generosity and in breadth of vision, with this Youth Seminar on World Religions which has been conceived and financed by Reverend Moon. A new related enterprise which he has recently initiated is the Religious Youth Service, in which young people from many faiths devote their time and energy to summer projects of relief and humanitarian service in developing countries.

Then there is the great series of "God Conferences," of which the stated theme is: "God: the Contemporary Discussion." Five of these international gatherings have been held in various parts of the world, bringing together many hundreds of scholars from all religions and countries to converse together about the most important of all subjects on which the human mind can dwell—namely, God. The results of these important colloquies have been published in several volumes.

But the initiative which, in my own experience, ranks highest of all, is the Council for the World's Religions. This Council was called into existence as the consequence of a decision by Reverend Moon in August 1984. It is the flowering and the fruit of all the other interfaith projects I have mentioned earlier. Linked with it, in his grand vision, is the series of quadrennial Assemblies of the World Religions.

The Council for the World's Religions is truly international and inter-religious. Its Consultative Board includes representatives from the Buddhist, Confucian, Christian, Hindu, Jewish, Muslim and Sikh faiths, as well as primal religion, and representatives from other faiths will join them soon. I believe the Council for the World's Religions is destined to be the main channel through which Reverend Moon's master plan for bringing together the religions of the world will be realized. The Council is working for the establishment of a permanent forum and meeting place for the world's religions. It looks forward to the day when all religions will be represented in a kind of "United Nations of Religions," working with a common mind and heart in the service of God for the welfare of mankind. I have

gladly pledged my whole-hearted support for this great venture, and I am dedicating most of my time, thought and energy to working for its success.

To prepare the way for that eventual objective, the first major Assembly of the World's Religions brought together over 700 men and women of all faiths and nations, in a plenary gathering in New Jersey, U.S.A., in November 1985. This manifestation of interfaith harmony and resolve was a religious and human event of the first magnitude. The week-long program was not only a global and intellectual dialogue, but also a spiritual, musical, artistic and social encounter between believers of the world. The 1985 Assembly was the first in a series which will culminate in a major celebration in 1993, on the centenary of the 1893 Chicago Parliament of Religions.

As well as preparing for these large Assemblies, the Council for the World's Religions has begun an extensive program of more specialized conferences. The objectives of the Council for the World's Religions are not only *inter*-religious but also *intra*-religious. That is, it seeks not only to bring different religions into harmony with one another, but also to promote internal harmony within each of the different world faiths. Reverend Moon, who knows (by his own experience of divided Christianity in Korea) how religion can be weakened by internal quarrels, wants the Council to foster reconciliation and mutual respect between the different traditions within all the world religions. So each year the Council organizes, in addition to its major interfaith conferences, a full program of intra-religious conferences in many lands.

All these manifold activities are part

of Reverend Moon's master plan for
harnessing the power of religion for
good on a global scale. It is a privilege
and a joy for me to collaborate in this
great enterprise for world religious
harmony.

Towards a Pluralistic Future: Prelude to World Peace

J. Deotis Roberts

I believe that the future of the human family must be open to diversity of religions and cultures. The resistance to tolerance in religious and cultural affairs can only be temporary if there is to be profound peace and cooperation among humans.

As I reflect upon the vision of the Reverend Sun Myung Moon, this affirmation of pluralism is in my judgement a great strength. It anticipates the way the religions of the world must travel if they are to be effective in healing the wounds of humanity. Intolerance and religious narrowness lead inevitably to strife and bitterness. When religions major in heresy trials, they lose their ability to be transformative in the moral sphere. Spiritual sterility and ethical weakness accompany religious intolerance.

I. Pluralism Does Not Negate Religious Commitment.

It is true that the Unification Church has its set of doctrines. These are based largely upon the spiritual conversion and life experience of Reverend Moon. Thus the context of the Korean experience of the movement explains much that is later developed in the life and thought of this Church. The Korean experience radiates throughout the life and thought of Unificationism. It explains not only the theology and ethics of the movement. The Korean experience is a clue to its pro-American, anti-Communist, familial and capitalistic tendencies.

There is much in the Unification Church which goes against my personal convictions and which contradicts my personal experience as a minority person in the United States. The recent ordeal of Reverend Moon in the United

States confirms many of the issues minorities have had to struggle with for hundreds of years in that setting. But the common experience of suffering, and the manner he has dealt with it prior to and during the recent court case and prison term, is reflective of a bond he has with minorities in their suffering. The religious response to suffering is to be lifted up.

So far we have argued that persons may have real differences in their religious convictions and yet share profound experiences which bring them together. I am convinced that the religious response to unmerited suffering is one of these. This brings the Exodus and the Cross together. This provides biblical and theological grounds for shared insights from Jews, Blacks and Koreans as they have dealt redemptively with the theme of suffering.

II. The Kingdom of Heaven on Earth.

The goal of Unificationism is the Kingdom of Heaven on earth. This goal is shared with Liberal Protestants. Indeed, it has been present as a significant aspiration for Christians throughout history. Most social utopian visions are mere derivatives of this Christian goal.

This vision is as persistent as *peace*. There has perhaps never been the absence of war in human history, and, yet, there has always been the longing for peace. Peace is something that humans are willing to work for. Indeed, because this is so, the world is a better place in which to live. In a similar way there is the human longing for the kingdom of Heaven on earth.

It is for this reason that many ministers find themselves working side by side with followers of Reverend Moon. We will mention just some of the pro-

grams. The Interdenominational Conferences for Clergy and the CAUSA Ministerial Alliance bring ministers of all denominations into discussions on pressing issues. The local Councils of the Church and Social Action actually feed the hungry. Those who minister to homeless and starving people view the Gospel as Good News to the poor and homeless masses. They do not spend time in a battle over the Bible and neither do they have the luxury of arguing over difficult points of doctrine. This explains why minority ministeries often work side by side with all groups who reach out to the weak and the needy.

III. Concern for Families

There is a concern for family life in the Unification Church which strikes a responsive cord among minorities. My personal concern for strong families among blacks has an echo in this movement. The history and social circumstances which explain the current crisis in families is different in each case. But the strong emphasis for the need to enrich and empower family life finds mutual expression. It is the humanitarian strand of Unification thought and life which warrants real attention.

One would need, however, to go deeper into the family model of Unificationism before adopting it as a norm. I have theological and pragmatic reservations about this view. But I affirm the importance of the family to human well-being. The attention given to family is worthwhile and should be appropriately taken up by all churches, religions, and groups interested in a wholesome human future.

IV. Contribution to Knowledge and Culture

As a person associated with New ERA from its inception, I find it to serve a noble purpose. It provides a forum for religious scholars of many religions and ideologies to learn and grow together. While it did provide exposure for Unification thought and opportunities for the development of Unification thinkers, the sharing of outsiders in fellowship, understanding and learning was a worthy outcome. Many non-Unification scholars have grown to great maturity through this network. There are some scholars who did not have the means or the opportunity for such development on their own and through the institutions they served.

Through the network of scholarly agencies initiated and supported by the Unification Church, scientists as well as scholars of religion and ethics have benefitted. Few persons of means, religious or otherwise, have done more to develop scholars, especially religious scholars, than Reverend Moon.

V. Questions of Religious Liberty

It was the trial of reverend Moon which raised forcefully the issue of religious freedom in the United States in recent history. Church-State relations as well as general questions of religious liberty have been raised to a higher level of visibility as a result of his trial and imprisonment.

Groups and denominations generally unfriendly to Reverend Moon and the Unification Church came to his support. Enlightened self-interest motivated many of these individuals and groups. But for most his treatment dealt with fundamental principles of religious liberty which merit attention in a free soci-

Dr. J. Deotis Robert at a banquet for local leaders, Tottori, Japan

ety. Thus the issues raised will claim the attention of religious bodies and the courts for years to come. This was an issue that begged for attention. The consequences of this event may go far beyond its original intention.

VI. Openness to Criticism

One real test for the commitment to pluralism comes when a movement subjects itself to analysis and rigorous criticism. Unificationism has opened itself to such criticism and has passed this test. In this way, it has established its high level of tolerance alluded to earlier. But, in addition, this openness to criticism has fostered growth in those who have been party to numerous dialogues sponsored by the Unification Church around the world. Persons have grown religiously, culturally and otherwise by the vision and outreach of Unificationism. Where the movement has received criticism, its members have been challenged to grow and learn to appreciate those holding very different opinions, and to overcome their own prejudices about others. The future effectiveness of the Church as a movement for unification depends upon its continued openness to new viewpoints and to receiving constructive criticism. As long as the Church continues to listen and respond to criticism, it will continue to be a positive and tolerant movement for good.

Personal Comment

The present writer is a Christian theologian. This means that his confessional stance is anchored in the theology of the Christian Church through the centuries with a strong Christological focus as stated in the Creeds.

I am at the same time a student of all cultures and all religions. My study, research and teaching of the great religions have become a part of my total outlook. Dialogue with religionists of many persuasions has enriched my outlook and deepened my understanding.

Finally, my concern is for better human understanding. One of the greatest threats of our time is religious fundamentalism. In the name of God and doctrinal purity, some of the cruellest crimes against humanity are being fostered. Thus I find common cause with those who are on the side of human understanding across racial, cultural and religious differences. Thus where there is dialogue and bridges of cooperation to enrich and enable human life I find some basic agreement. This does not mean for me a radical change in religious outlook. For me a worthy understanding of God includes a concern for life's meaning and the quest for social justice.

Under the Umbrella: The Reverend Sun Myung Moon's Goal and Strategy for the Unification of Christianity and the Other World Religions

Richard Quebedeaux

The ecumenical goal of the Unification Church, described by the movement's corporate name—the Holy Spirit Association for the Unification of World Christianity (HSA-UWC)—has been obscured, and is unknown to most people, who are aware of the Unification Church and its members only through the negative stereotypes of the popular media. Yet religious harmony has been a central concern of the Unification Church ever since its founding in South Korea in 1954, and the movement has always spent a substantial portion of its total budget on ecumenical Christian and interreligious programs. This activity began to take on international significance, however, only after Reverend Moon moved from Korea to New York in December 1971.

The purpose of this essay is to trace the development of Reverend Moon's U.S.-based ecumenical projects since 1975, discuss his strategy and ultimate goal for the "wider ecumenism," and assess his prospects for success in the midst of modern secular society.

A Program for Unification

The stage was set for the development of Reverend Moon's ecumenical projects in the U.S. with his founding of the Unification Theological Seminary (UTS) in Barrytown, New York, in September 1975. The seminary was modeled after the great ecumenical graduate schools like Union Theological Seminary, Harvard and Yale Divinity Schools, giving its faculty a great deal of academic freedom, and subjecting its students—all members of the Unification Church—to the *critical* study of theology, the Bible, other scriptures, even the teachings of Reverend Moon himself. For such a young movement (then only 21 years old) to establish a school of this sort was unprecedented, but even more surprising was the fact that Reverend Moon staffed the faculty not primarily with Unification Church members, but with professors from a wide variety of Christian traditions and from a few other religions as well—Protestant, Catholic, Greek Orthodox, Jewish, and Confucianist. Only one professor, Dr. Young Oon Kim, was a member of the Unification Church. David S.C. Kim, one of Reverend Moon's earliest and most ecumenical disciples, became president of UTS, and created an ethos there in the ensuing years highly conducive to Christian ecumenical and interreligious activities.

Part of the UTS budget was designated for the development of a seminary-based ecumenical program. During the first few years of its operation, the seminary invited a number of eminent ecumenically-oriented theologians to give lectures on their fields at Barrytown. But, beginning in 1977, the focus would be on small conferences with outside scholars and seminary students. Dr. Herbert Richardson, a professor of theology at the University of Toronto, had read and took a liking to *Divine Principle,* Sun Myung Moon's "new revelation." Because of this interest, he brought together some of his former doctoral students at Barrytown in January 1977 for a weekend gathering with an equal number of UTS seminarians. This was the first seminary conference on Unification theology; and, under the leadership of Professor Darrol Bryant of the University of Waterloo in Canada, similar small conferences for North American religion scholars were held on a regular basis at UTS each year from then on.

In June 1978, I convened the first formal dialogue between two specific schools of religious thought in the series. It was a conference on the differences between evangelical theology and Unification theology, and included a number of evangelical Christian leaders among the participants. A second seminar was held in October 1978, followed by several other dialogues with evangelical theologians which ran parallel to the more general conferences on Unification theology moderated by Dr. Bryant. Some of these gatherings were so novel and so interesting (due partly to the major controversy surrounding the Unification Church at the time) that it was decided to publish transcripts of them as books; and, in 1978, UTS founded its own publishing program (Rose of Sharon Press, Inc.) to take on this responsibility.

By the spring of 1979, it had become clear to Reverend Moon that these ecumenical conferences on Unification theology constituted one of the most successful things his church was doing. They were changing theologians' minds about the Unification Church, and were giving the church's budding young theologians (the best UTS graduates were now pursuing doctoral work at Harvard, Yale, Columbia, and elsewhere) an opportunity to test and witness to their faith in dialogue with highly critical religion scholars. Thus, the conference budget was increased significantly, enabling the organizers to plan larger seminars, some of which were held in luxury resort hotels. In August 1979, the first week-long introductory seminar on Unification theology was gathered in the Virgin Islands, and this was followed in February 1980 by two advanced conferences on specific topics coming out of the introductory seminar.

To supervise and coordinate the growing number of theological conferences and publications related to them, the New Ecumenical Research Association (New ERA) was established in the spring of 1980, with Dr. Bryant and myself as staff consultants, and a number of theologians who had been active in the previous seminars serving three-year terms as advisors to the organization.

Thus far, the Unification Church-sponsored ecumenical conference program had centered its interests on the assessment and critique of Unification theology per se; but, beginning in 1980, seminars on broader cultural and religious themes were initiated, including an annual conference on the sociology of religion, and seminars on topics ranging from family values to hermeneutics' from death and immortality to socialism and religion. Conferences also took on an international and more interreligious (rather than just intra-Christian) character. In December 1981, the first annual conference on "God: The Contemporary Discussion" took place in Hawaii, involving more than a hundred scholars from over thirty nations and virtually all religions, with Unification theology taking its place as one religion among many.

By the end of 1981, a pattern had been established by New ERA for the conduct of its seminars that would also characterize those conducted by other Unification-sponsored ecumenical programs. In the beginning, it had been very difficult to get theologians to attend—given the negativity surrounding *anything* hosted by the Unification movement. But by the time of the first

Dr. Richard Quebedeaux

"God conference," some of the most eminent theologians in the world were participating in New ERA seminars along with the increasingly sophisticated Unification graduate students, and were contributing to the project's books.

From the start, all the conferences— even those on Unification theology— were especially intriguing to scholars because of the openness of the participants and Unification hosts who evaluated even their own theology in a self-critical manner. In an environment of care and mutual respect, free discussion and engaging dialogue could come about. Theological and religious disagreements could be expressed without acrimony and bitterness. Inevitably, friendships formed among people of different Christian persuasions and of different religions—among scholars in the same disciplines who would have never even met except in these circumstances. New ERA "fellow travelers" have tended to be creative mavericks and risk-takers who were not terribly concerned about what other people thought of their association with the "Moonies." They have been "free thinkers" who, because of their independence and forthrightness, created an intellecutally stimulating environment. (Many of them have also been prominent in their own professional societies such as the American Academy of Religion and the Society for the Scientific Study of Religion.) And since they represented only themselves, not their churches or academic institutions, they were free to express their opinions as they saw fit, without respect to the official positions of their respective organizations. Most importantly, New ERA was organized by "outside" scholars *themselves,* and could thus fulfill the specific needs and desires of the academic community they represented.

On the basis of the growing association of professors involved with New ERA, Reverend Moon initiated other interreligious projects of a similar character. In 1982, the first Youth Seminar on World Religions (YSWR) took place. Each summer through 1985, more than a hundred young professionals and graduate students in their twenties, and from many religious traditions, have made a global pilgrimage to religious homelands around the world. Also in 1982, the Sun Myung Moon Institute (SMMI) was founded and has sponsored conferences for scholars on the themes of East-West relations in general and Pacific Basin studies in particular.

Then, in 1985, the first of three "Assemblies of the World's Religions" was held under Unification auspices. Modeled after the 1893 Parliament of the World's Religions in Chicago, this Assembly gathered some 600 religious leaders and scholars from 85 nations for a week of discussions, plenary addresses from representatives of many religions—far more than in the Chicago Parliament—religious ceremonial and meditative events, and the like. The next two Assemblies (1989 and 1993) will be supervised by the newly established (1985) Council for the World's Religions (CWR) with advisors from the major religions. The Council is currently sponsoring a series of "intra-religious" conferences which seek to promote unity within each of the world's religions.

Concurrently with its ecumenical work with theologians and professors of religion, the Unification movement had been engaging in ecumenical outreach to Christian clergy. In 1982, The Interdenominational Conferences for Clergy (ICC) began, and they have been held for clergy and lay leaders at sites in the Caribbean and throughout the United States.

All of these aforementioned ecumenical and interreligious activities which emerged from the New ERA experience are now organized under the International Religious Foundaton (IRF), incorporated in 1983 in New York. The IRF is a tax-exempt foundation, staffed by members of the Unification Church who organize all the events sponsored by New ERA, the Youth Seminar, the Sun Myung Moon Institute, the Assembly of World Religions the Council for the World Religions, and the Interdenominational Conferences for the Clergy. Its chairman and president, the Reverend Chung Hwan Kwak, was an early disciple of Reverend Moon, and the Unification Church underwrites all of its expenses. Conference participants are informed about past and future events in the bimonthly *IRF Newsletter,* which began in 1980 as the *New ERA Newsletter.* IRF publishes some of the best offerings from its conferences in a scholarly journal, *Dialogue and Alliance.* And books deriving from IRF seminars are now published under the "New ERA Books" imprint by Paragon House, a newly-organized publisher of scholarly books.

Thus, in less than a decade, Reverend Moon has been able to establish his own ecumenical movement, administered by the IRF, and centered on theological conferences and scholarly publications deriving from those seminars. Unlike the World Council of Churches, IRF-sponsored gatherings are interreligious and not just intra-Christian in nature; and participants from the various world religions represent their traditions only as private individuals, not as "official delegates" from religious hierarchies. They are free to speak for themselves. Furthermore, no effort is made to invite only "orthodox" representatives from the traditions; "heretics" of all opinions are welcome at these conferences. Given the scope of IRF ecumenical activities, the thousands of theologians and ministers who have participated in them over the years—and still identify with the work—and the millions of dollars spent by the sponsor on these international projects each year, Reverend Moon and the Unification Church have already done ecumenically what no other church or religion has ever done. Indeed, each organized activity—by its very nature and the scope of its participants—has been a groundbreaking event.

Ecumenical Goal and Strategy

What, then, is Reverend Moon's precise goal in his ecumenical and interreligious endeavors, and how does he expect to accomplish it? Reverend Moon feels that, in the short run, people are influenced most by the mass media; but in the long run, intellectuals—who manipulate the symbols of understanding in specific societies—have the most impact. Among intellectuals, then, theologians (and ministers) represent the "spinal cord" of the human population—developing and promoting in their scholarship and teaching the core values by which people live and society is run. Therefore, Reverend Moon feels that the constructive work of intellectuals should be supported by his movement.

Furthermore, to a degree unmatched by any other religious body, the Unification Church seeks, as an ideal, to put the largest part of the movement's material and human resources at the disposal of *other* churches and religions. By serving and even sacrificing for them, by raising the money to host theologians and clergy at expensive conferences—and befriending them in the process—members of the Unification Church are seen to "indemnify" the historic resentments that are the major cause of division among the world's religions. Reverend Moon believes that when religious scholars and ministers are served in such a way, their antagonism toward the serving host *and* each other will be replaced—through genuine dialogue and give-and-take—with a feeling of tolerance and respect, even for those with theological and other differences, and with a new willingness to work together for the common good despite those differences.

As theologians discuss their concerns in conferences sponsored by the Unification Church, they will want to give something back—and this is a basic assumption of his strategy. The sacrifice and service rendered by the Unification Church will not go unrewarded. But *what* does he want from these scholars? For Reverend Moon, there are three major obstacles to the realization of God's reign in the world. The first is increasing immorality—due to extremely self-centered love. Immorality is understood here as a lack of respect for and commitment to others and things, resulting in serious social problems. The second obstacle is disunity—not only between nations, races, and cultures, but also between religions. Throughout history, religions which have professed the same God, similar teachings and values, have found themselves persecuting and warring with

each other, engaging in intolerance, bigotry, and religious triumphalism. Third and finally is the obstacle of atheistic communism, with its denial of God and God's goodness, and its often totalitarian methods restricting human freedom.

Unlike many religious leaders in the Western world, Reverend Moon genuinely believes that—as the world's spinal cord—theologians and ministers can be the key to eradicating these three obstacles to God's reign on earth. He feels certain that in honest, caring dialogue with each other, and through the living example of Unification Church members who—in fundraising and actual participation—make that dialogue possible, the values and attitudes of theologians and ministers will be transformed to the point that their scholarship will reflect the change, and thus be more convincing and effective. Reverend Moon does not tell the scholars hosted at IRF conferences *how* to pay him back, or even that they must (and this unconditional stance very much appeals to Western intellectuals so often defensive about their automony and right not to conform.) Nor does he tell them they have to join the Unification Church. Rather, it is his assumption—rooted in Unification theology—that by receiving the movement's generosity, and in association with its sacrificial members, they will, ultimately, reflect and pursue his values from their *own* religions, as "Unificationist" Protestants, Catholics, Muslims, Jews, or whatever, who work together ecumenically, toward the same goal, under the Unification "umbrella."

Prospects for Success

All this constitutes Reverend Moon's goal and strategy for his interreligious quest. But will he succeed? With respect to fostering religious "unity" Reverend Moon has already accomplished a great deal by bringing together in regular conversation representative scholars of the widest variety of religions and by publishing their views. Although leaders of the established Christian denominations and religious hierarchies of the world initially stayed away from the seminars—in an effort not to "legitimate" the Unification Church—this opposition has been gradually decreasing, and we can probably expect further weakening of this "boycott" in the future.

As to Reverend Moon's desire for intellectuals to help improve the world's moral climate, the best he can hope for has already begun to happen—seminars for theologians and ministers from a wide socio-cultural background on pressing social and ethical concerns, from family values to apartheid, in which these issues are debated and the results published. In the conferences, participants have at least come to appreciate many of Reverend Moon's specific social concerns, if not agree with some of them.

As of yet, however, Reverend Moon's evaluation of Communism (Marxism-Leninism) as a "satanic" enemy to be defeated with the help of religious intellectuals has not readily appealed to most of the scholars under the IRF umbrella. Many of them prefer socialism as a morally superior economic system to capitalism, and some even accept a generally Marxian analysis of class and society. Their objections have been apparent at almost all IRF-sponsored conferences—in which a number of

scholars have stood in vigorous opposition to what they see as Reverend Moon's seemingly too "conservative" political stance on international Communism. Of course, Reverend Moon has set up other organizations, notably CAUSA and the *Washington Times*, to involve political scientists and intellectuals in the fight against Communism, and these have been quite successful. Nevertheless, he continues to try, through IRF conferences, to make his position persuasive for theologians and religious scholars as well. He seems confident that, ultimately, through further dialogue and association, they, too, will understand and accept his view of the danger of Communism. This confidence comes in part from his view that the alternative to Communism is to be found in a vision of the world in which religion plays a central role.

Thus in only a few short years, Reverend Moon has made a substantial impact on the world religious scene through various ecumenical projects. Besides generating good-will and some understanding for his much-maligned and misunderstood church, they have already made a significant contribution towards the work of ecumenical and interreligious dialogue. They have also challenged theologians and clergy to take seriously the problems of immorality in modern society and the threat of Communism. As these projects continue to develop, I expect further progress, particularly towards the primary goal of ecumenical and interreligious harmony and unity to which people of all religions aspire.

THREE

SCIENCE
AND SPIRITUAL
VALUES

Unification in Physics and Spirituality

Jean Charon

I met Reverend Sun Myung Moon in 1979. Today, I should acknowledge the fact that Reverend Moon appears now to me as the most "creative" person that I have had the privilege to know. Reverend Moon looked to me "creative" through his direct and active participation to our world and through his efficient and obstinate will to help this world to evolve towards more justice, more well-being, more peace, more harmony. This goes from the International Highway crossing a large part of the East to the setting up of the World Peace Academy, to that wonderful School of the "Little Angels" in Seoul. My colleagues are certainly going to speak in great details of those realizations of Reverend Moon, and since I am myself only a physicist, specialized in what is called "Unification theories," I am going to limit myself here to what looks to me as an important aspect of Reverend Moon's thought, an aspect which is directly related to a preoccupation right at the center of contemporary Physics: precisely, unification theories.

Let us first briefly recall that Physics distinguishes four types of interactions: weak and strong at the nuclear and particle level, electromagnetic for phenomena related to light and gravitational for attraction between celestial bodies. Unification in Physics means to demonstrate that these four interactions are different aspects of the same fundamental reality: in other words, Unification has for its objective to show that, in spite of an apparent (and fortunate) large diversity, there is a fundamental basic Unity of our world. Until very recently Physics had practically unified three of the four interactions, only gravitational was still left out. This last unifying step is, however, as I shall explain, being hopefully accomplished now. It has some important consequences for our vision of the world.

One particular thought of Reverend Moon has, since my first encounter with him, deeply impressed me: the idea that the "substance" of our Universe should be represented through both material and spiritual dimensions, these two dimensions showing *both* a true "existence," that is, a right to be considered as truly existing. According to Reverend Moon, this complementary aspect of our universe should some day be directly represented by science, not only "soft" science, but also "hard" science. And the well-known ICUS annual meetings have been organized in part to encourage such a research.

What I wish to stress here is that this premonitory statement from Reverend Moon has practically already become today a *reality* in Physics. The more this scientific discipline was progressing towards Unification, the more it became apparent that the representation of matter should include, starting at the smallest scale, memorizing and ordering properties. To be true, physicists do not yet qualify these properties of matter as "spiritual" but rather call them "mental" properties, but we definitely are on the way.

I do not plan to give here a lecture in Physics, but however I think that I could not do better to illustrate Reverend Moon's thinking than to briefly summarize how Physics of our century has been led, in order to get an always more "complete" representation of our outer world, to start speaking in some way of our "inner" world.

As it is often the case in the history of science, a large step forward in the representation of our world was accomplished at the moment when physicists gave up their spontaneously anthropocentrist attitude and accepted that the world might, after all, contain features that "exist" although they are not directly "visible." And by the word "visible" we here mean features which are not directly "extended" in our three dimensional "usual" space. A good example is a "thought:" a thought has an exitence, no doubt about this, however you cannot locate it in any part of space. To take into account such "invisible" features it becomes necessary to assume that the world actually contains more than its pure materialistic visible aspect, and that we should consequently make provisions to become able to represent, in science, "existing although invisible" characteristics. And we should assume this possibility at the smallest dimensional scale, that is at the level of those "elementary" particles (protons, electrons...) that compose the very "substance" of everything in our universe. Let us see how this transition between two drastically different approaches (materialistic and material-spiritual) has been progressively achieved in Physics during our century.

1. 1880-1915: Electromagnetism and Relativity

This is the purely "materialistic" period. The particle of matter looks for physi-

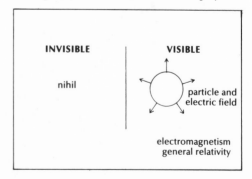

cists as a kind of "billiard ball" from which can eventually emerge an electric field (charged particle).

Einstein proposed that the universe is entirely made of continuous "substance", which is called space-time. The particle of matter itself can be considered as a local "compactification" of this substance. *Nothing* is assumed to be "invisible," since only space "exists" around us, and that space is an extended "continuum," completely "visible" by definition.

Dr. Jean Charon
speaking in a suburb
of Seoul, Korea

2. 1915-1950: Quantum Theory and the Wave Aspect

Physicists then discovered that the image of the "billiard ball" is an incomplete representation of the individual particle of matter. Some wave character has to be associated to the particle. Curiously enough, however, this wave, which is usually called the "psi wave," is a "subjective" wave; it seems not to belong to the particle itself, and not to propagate in the visible space, but to be there only to help "the observer" of the particle to obtain indications related to the position of the moving particle in space.

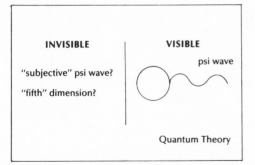

We would be tempted to say that the true entrance of the "invisible" in Physics takes place with this apparently inevitable "subjective" connection between the particle and the observer's mind processes.

During the same period the Russian physicist Kaluza gets the idea "that there might be more in the world than has been dreaming Einstein's philosophy" (Hamlet). And he suggests to put that "more" into an additional "fifth" dimension. Should this new dimension be considered as another clue to the existence of the invisible part of the universe?

3. 1950-1970: Non-Abelian Gauge Theories and the Point-Like Aspect

The picture of the particle is now becoming both simplified and more sophisticated. Experimental and theoretical evidence have shown that what seems truly "elementary" in the individual particle are "point-like" structures, with no extension whatsoever in space (like a true mathematical point, of volume zero). These points with no extension (quarks, gluons, leptons, etc.) can obviously no longer be *geometrically* represented. Physicists use for their description purely abstract features, choosing words to designate such features with no directly "visible" meanings like strangeness, charm, beauty, top, bottom... Physicists also look for non-geometrical "symmetries" between these abstract features.

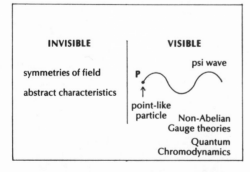

However, a non trivial question soon comes up in Physics: since we are now

left in the "visible" space with only point-like (hence invisible) particles, each particle being itself associated with a purely "subjective" (hence also invisible) psi wave, where and how should we represent the world ("what is")? Should we say that the visible is completely invisible? And that the only "reality," the only "substance," is finally what Physics had so far called the "invisible" (i.e. "not worth being studied by an objective science like Physics")?

4. 1970 up to now: Hidden Dimensions Theories

Here we come back to Kaluza's idea that the world is still probably more complex than what Einstein had brought with his relativistic revolution. Since it is no longer possible to geometrically represent in the "visible" the individual particles of matter, and since these particles must however be extended "somewhere," the logical conclusion was to assume that these particles were extending *in the invisible part* of the world: the world now construed as both visible and invisible. This idea was drastically new for a science which had long pretended that she was an exact science, and precisely "exact" because it took only into account what was "observable," that is directly visible. Physicists were at last opening a window on the invisible part of our universe. They more modestly started accepting that they lived in a world which was not purely material (visible), and that they should use more than their "outer" eyes, but also their "inner" eyes, to get a more complete image of the place in which they were born.

The main objective of Physics in recently developing in this way what are called "hidden dimensions" theories has been primarily to obtain a more *complete* and more *unified* representation of the physical phenomena, that is of the four known physical interactions (weak, strong, electromagnetic, and gravitational). Such tentatives are, for example, the unification proposed by the Nobel laureate Abdus Salam with his Supergravity, or the unified theory of the American physicist John Schwarz with his Superstring. The proposed number of additional (and invisible) dimensions varies with each theory; it is generally six or seven, making in this way a total of ten or eleven dimensions for our universe when we add to the "visible" four dimensions the "invisible" part of the world.

We have tried to "picture" such hidden dimensions theories in the illustration above. The plane in the illustration represents the geometry of the "visible" space-time, which on a large scale is nearly flat; coordinate lines along one axis represent space and coordinate lines along the second perpendicular axis represents time. The *surfaces* of the spheres shown at the intersection of the coordinates lines represent the "hidden" dimensions postulated by the new theories. Obviously, the illustration can only suggest the appearance of the structure;

the spheres bearing the invisible part of the world should be imagined as tangent to the plane *at every point* of the quasi-flat visible space. Moreover, in the illustration the spheres and the plane actually give rise to only four dimensions, instead of ten and eleven respectively in the theories of Schwarz and Salam.

In such representations we consequently accept that each point of our visible space is the point-like "trace" of an "invisible" region of the total universe which needs additional dimensions to be geometrically located and represented. With such a representation Schwarz and Salam have nearly succeeded to unify three of the four physical interactions (gravitational still out).

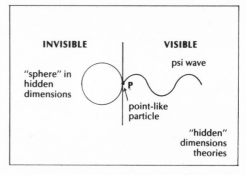

In my own work, which is called Complex Relativity (four hidden dimensions only), we have for the first time obtained the unification of *all four* physical interactions. The "spheres" in the hidden dimensions are, in Complex Relativity, closed micro-universes made of matter, light and neutrinos ("strong" black holes). A distinction is made between "eons" (charged particle) and "preons" (neutral particle)[1].

We should immediately mention that one very special new feature characterizes Complex Relativity: the total unification of the four interactions is

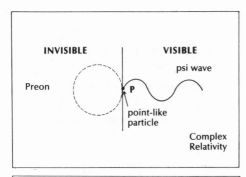

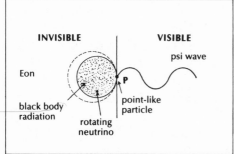

memorizing and ordering properties. In other words, according to Complex Relativity *each individual particle* should from now on be considered as a kind of "psychomatter," and no more as a crude material "billiard ball" as it was still accepted some few years ago in the purely "materialistic" representation proposed by Physics. Unification has brought with her the discovery of "mind properties" to be associated to each point of our universe.

This is probably the first *scientific* approach to a more "spiritualistic" vision of our world. When reaching at the deepest of their investigation of matter, physicists have finally been reflecting their own visage. Again, towards this direction of progress, Reverend Sun Myung Moon has been pointing the way.

obtained if (and only if) we assume that the new invisible spheres located in the four hidden dimensions are filled up with a black body radiation (practically, a special form of light) which, according to its mathematical representation, has

Note
1. See Jean E. Charon, *Complex Relativity: Unifying All Four Physical Interactions* (New York: Paragon House Publishers, 1987).

A Foundation for Dialogue Between Science and Philosophy

Nona R. Bolin

Contemporary society has produced a uniquely new set of philosophical problems which center about complex issues of science and technology. In the past the uncertainty of the physical world bred an insecurity such that man strove for some measure of control over the environment. In the West the increased control was conjoined with an increased domination of all that was considered external and threatening to human existence, reducing the world to the composite of mere consumable and expandable "things." Science and technology came to be the ultimate weapons in the war for domination and acquisition, but these supposed "solutions" that were the offspring of the ascendancy of control have now engendered new problems that are themselves the by-products of the folly of mastery.

For the Reverend Sun Myung Moon, founder of the International Conference on the Unity of the Sciences, "Our attitude which tends to over-emphasize the value of science may need re-examination."[1] According to the Reverend Moon, science must not be conceived as an end in itself. Thus the illusion of mastery propagated by what has often times been called "pure science" must be called into question. The privilege that science has all too often claimed for itself has any number of dangers. The horrors of Hiroshima and the concentration camps of Europe have taught us that science can be manipulated for the service of nationalism, racism and sexism. The fiction of "pure science" may also serve to blind specialists and intellectuals to the human consequences of their work. This threat undermines the very interests of the scientific activity and makes legitimate research suspect. The Reverend Moon is concerned that

Dr. Nona Bolin

science retain its original goal, namely, the happiness of all mankind. He says: "...scientists have developed science and technology with a keen sense of mission to actualize the dreams of mankind. Sometimes the results of scientific research have been misused by men of power for unrighteous purposes, but still the fundamental spirit of scientists has aimed towards the fulfillment of an ideal society for man."[2]

The myth of "pure science" has two predominant forms. The first form derives its plausibility from the classical divisions of *theoria* and *techne*. It is grounded in a rationalism that maintains that the Real and the Ideal are antecedently fixed and final, irreparably separated from the material world of appearance and flux. Thus rational inquiry engages in an unbiased search for knowledge and seeks its answers within the realm of a closed universe. The goal of this knowledge is certainty, at least in principle. But this certainty can only be guaranteed by the ontological separation of the world of the actual and the world of appearance. The world of the actual is the world of essences and forms in classical thought, which is penetrable by means of the elevated faculty of human reason. This is the domain of "pure science." The mundane world of appearance is the world of sense knowledge, the practical world that has been devalued throughout the history of the West. This is the domain of technology or "applied science," a lesser pursuit followed by those whose work is not so elevated. The inquiry of the "pure scientist" is to gain certain knowledge, out of which man may gain security and the complete mastery of nature. The research of the "applied scientist" yields only particular facts which are useful for only proximate ends.

This distinction between "pure science" and "applied science" lingers in our thought even today, long after Darwin and Einstein. It is a distinction that is not benign. We find its consequences in the very fabric of our social and political lives, in our relations with others, and rooted in the ways in which we regard ourselves and our world. Those who are concerned with so-called "higher" pursuits demand a superior social status, presumably distinct and isolated from those concerned with technology and its applications. Divisions of labor, economic rewards and social prestige center about the desire for certainty, and those who promise such certainty benefit from the rewards of power.

The second form of the myth of "pure science" demands that the pursuit of the Real remain the business of those who conform to the standards that have already been established by those favored by the system. Knowledge of the "Real" is the possession of an all too often insular group who remain unaffected by the inquiries of other disciplines. These other disciplines are often dismissed as less rigorous or informed. The uniqueness of the subject matter of "pure science" leaves its inquiry singular and narcissistic. It is presumed that the findings of "pure science" impact on all other areas of knowledge, but, outside the matrix of the specializations integral to its concerns, all other pursuits make little or no difference.

Science, according to the Reverend Moon, is a secondary level of inquiry. Such a conception of science already questions the possibility of its purity. His theology maintains an open universe wherein revelation is not closed. For him, science arises within a social context and is pursued for a social purpose—the happiness of all mankind. Reciprocally, science impacts on our everyday lives. Thus the separation of facts and values is as fictitious as the division between pure and practical science. We can no longer afford to regard science as a collection of unconstable ideas backed up by the authority of those who have a privileged relation to "Reality." Science can no longer linger in the luxury of separating itself from the all too human tasks of practical living. Scientists must become involved in the human community and take no inquiry as irrelevant to the emergence of new knowledge, even if that knowledge seriously challenges its foundations. At a time when the risks are so great, science cannot be unconcerned with the mundane. Those dichotomies must be left to the past. Science must take responsibility for the technology on which it thrives, for better or for worse.

Neither can science maintain its value neutrality. This is not to say that science and technology are intrisically good or evil. Certainly the Reverend Moon has great faith that they can be greatly beneficial for the good of all. To say that they are not value neutral is to say that they are consequential. They are capable of transforming the world and our experience thereof toward certain desirable ends. These ends-in-view are never the sole property of any one nation, religion, tradition, group, or institution. They are the projections of what constitutes human happiness, and it is this point that concerns the Reverend Moon. He sees the possibility of dialogue amongst those who are concerned with the well-being of all who inhabit this world. He is so concerned that scientists from all over the world have an opportunity to speak to each other, and likewise others outside the scientific community, that he has provided a new and unique space for such dialogue to flourish. It is his conviction that scientists must have this opportunity in order that the pressing problems of the world be addressed by a convocation of scholars who represent the various concerns of the world's people.

In addressing the Eighth International Conference on the Unity of the Sciences the Reverend Moon stated that there is "a limit to science in its search for truth... In the twentieth century, science has finally found itself pushed into the realm of philosophy in its own search for truth."[3] Nevertheless, the privilege that once was claimed for "pure science" should not be transferred to any of the narrowly delimited understandings of academic philosophy, and the Reverend Moon would be the first to caution us about such a move. His words must strike a cord with philosophers as well as scientists; for that matter, with any group who would understand themselves to be the keepers of the Truth. Especially in the twentieth century, philosophy has practiced sharpening its cognitive skills often times at the expense of using them to resolve serious social problems. Professional *hubris* can find its place in any group, and it is often disguised in the claim of value neutrality. Much contemporary philosophy understands itself within the tradition of *theoria*, and proclaims immunity to the social context within which it is framed. Philosophy has its own history of ignoring the crucially problematic questions by insisting,

in its own way, on the fact/value dichotomy.

Reverend Moon serves as a constant reminder that we must all overcome our smugness and our narrowness and even be open to calling into question the institutions and the traditions within which we carry out our disciplinary inquiries. He has given many of us a new forum wherein new possibilities for dialogue are possible. Through his conferences, scholars have the occasion to converse with one another in ways that allow the dignity of their differences and the harmony of their commonalities. In an effort to overcome the alienation and fragmentation of knowledge all too often endentured to the nation, the culture or even to the university, the Reverend Moon reminds us that in order to pursue our own happiness we must first learn to listen to others, to learn from them, to inquire into their values and their goals. Then our own quest for happiness will take on what the Reverend Moon calls "Heart."

Creation is, for the Reverend Moon, the result of God's heart. Scholars must learn ro create and not simply produce. He says: "Through our amazing scientific progress we have begun to take after God's creative power, but not yet His love. In order to take after His love, we must practice love, and lead a life of goodness."[4]

The peace of the world, what the Reverend Moon understands to be the Kingdom of God on earth, will come about only through love, unselfish love. When each nation overcomes its own self-serving interests and begins to serve other nations, when its people are united in a love that reaches out across differences while still nurturing those differences, the peace of mankind will be a securable end. In our time, when we are so hazardously situated at the brink of destruction by our own hands and in the name of our own science, the Reverend Moon has much to give. And the most precious gift of all is his heart.

Notes

1. Sun Myung Moon, *Science and Absolute Values, Ten addresses by Sun Myung Moon* (New York: International Cultural Foundation, 1982) p. 26.

2. *Ibid.,* p. 3.

3. *Ibid.,* p. 83.

4. *Ibid.,* p. 9.

Some Applications of Unification Thought to the Problems of Ecology

Gene G. James

Modern science and technology have brought about vast improvements in the lives of individuals. But technology has not been an unmixed blessing. Indeed, there is a growing ecological crisis which is in large part the result of modern technology. Pollution, radiation from nuclear fallout, acid rain, the destruction of rain forests, the eradication of species which have existed for millions of years and other irreversible ecological changes are radically transforming the environment in which previous human life has taken place. These problems along with others such as the depletion of scarce natural resources, overpopulation and the possibility of nuclear holocaust threaten the destruction of humanity itself.

Because of the magnitude of the problems facing us, it is the belief of Reverend Sun Myung Moon that "solutions... cannot be arrived at through the efforts of any particular individual, group or country."[1] Only a world-wide cooperative effort will be capable of solving the problems which confront us.

Furthermore, science and technology have been employed mainly to gain private profit from the exploitation of nature or to subdue fellow human beings. Although scientists have usually been motivated by a desire to improve the human condition, "the results of scientific research have been misused by men of power for unrighteous purposes."[2] What is required is a change both in the way we think about nature and in the way we relate to our fellow human beings.

First, human beings must overcome egoism and selfishness that lead to war and exploitation. It is natural for people to be concerned for their own happiness and to wish their family, friends and

Dr. Gene G. James
in Kumamoto, Japan

nation to prosper. But Reverend Moon believes that human beings can achieve happiness only by giving to others without any desire to receive anything in return.[3] Egoism and selfishness condition can be overcome only if we adopt a theocentric way of life. Such a way of life requires that we value the good of humanity above that of ourself, our group, or our nation. In the context of the ecological crisis this requires that we seek world-wide solutions to problems even when these are not in the direct interest of our own nation. Reverend Moon believes that this is true for at least two reasons. First, because the problems are world-wide. They do not affect a few individuals or a few nations only, but threaten all of us. Second, because "in God's sight there are no national boundaries",[4] just human beings all of whom he loves equally.

The foregoing may be summed up by saying that according to Reverend Moon the solution to our ecological problems requires that we both change the way we think and feel toward our fellow human beings and seek international cooperation in solving the problems.

Solutions to the problems must begin with changes in the way people think and behave because the ecological crisis is an outward manifestation of an inward situation. "The sickness of ... society lies within the very essence of man's being."[5] Our problems can be solved, therefore, only if we overcome our fallen nature by adopting a theocentric philosophy of life.

Second, nationalistic divisions among humankind must be overcome. This cannot be done by one nation conquering the others. "If we make one world by conquering other nations, we will never have a peaceful or happy world."[6] People who believe that world unity can occur by the imposition of an ideology such as communism are mistaken because "to... bring about world unity, it is necessary to respect the value of the view of other people."[7] World unity can also not come about as long as there is economic exploitation of some people and nations by others. In order for humanity to become one there cannot be "any competition... because of excessive production, nor any accumulation or excessive consumption which would bring obstruction to the... life of the whole due to unfair distribution."[8] Reverend Moon has therefore recently proposed that "we need to establish a new international economic body so that we can avoid the extensive economic waste and loss of the past, and push forward a new land use plan... in order to endow all humanity with the right to enjoy peace and happiness."[9] He has also proposed the building of an international highway which would help bring about an integrated, equitable world economy.

Utilizing science and technology for the good of humanity rather than for selfish and nationalistic purposes will not be sufficient to improve the human condition unless we also change the way we think about nature in employing science and technology. Divine Principle, as Reverend Moon conceives it, does not apply to human relations only, but "applies also to the relationship between man and nature."[10] Nature was created by God who then felt joy in contemplating its beauty. Because human beings are created in God's image, they also have the capacity to feel joy in contemplating the beauty of nature. Nature was also created to serve humankind's material needs. Since nature was given to human beings to enjoy and to utilize for the satisfaction of material needs, humans may be said to be the center of creation.[11] However, this blessing which God bestowed on human beings necessitates gratitude and responsible action on the part of humans in interacting with nature. Human beings were given dominion over nature, not to exploit it for selfish purposes, but to preserve its beauty and to cultivate and utilize it for the common good. Humans should not be thought of as opposed to or outside of nature, but as a part of nature. Humans exist in a reciprocal relationship with the rest of nature.[12] The proper attitude of human beings toward nature requires that we both appreciate and preserve its beauty and utilize it for the common good. However, neither of these is possible without careful study of the ways human interactions with nature transform it. We must give much more attention than in past times to the reciprocal relationships of give and take between humans and nature, to the development of the science of ecology.

In addition, the limited perspectives of individual sciences must also give way to a unified science concerned with the total human environment: social, political and natural. This is one of the reasons Reverend Moon sponsors the International Conferences for the Unity of the Sciences. Although science and religion have in the past often been hostile to one another, this need not be true. Religious inspiration and scientific knowledge can complement one another. Surely Reverend Moon is right that if they are not in unison in the future we will be unable to solve our ecological problems. Only a combination of love and knowledge can be adequate to meet the crisis.

Notes

1. Sun Myung Moon, *Science and Absolute Values* (New York: International Cultural Foundation, 1982), p. 25.

2. *Ibid.*, p. 3.

3. Sun Myung Moon, *New Hope: Twelve Talks by Sun Myung Moon* (New York: HSA-UWC, 1982), pp. 87f., 93.

4. *Ibid.*, p. 79.

5. *Science and Absolute Values*, p. 34.

6. *New Hope*, p. 60.

7. *Ibid.*, p. 77.

8. *Divine Principle* (New York: HSA-UWC, 1977), p. 444.

9. *Science and Absolute Values*, pp. 109-10.

10. *New Hope*, p. 54.

11. *Divine Principle*, p. 58 ff.

12. *Ibid.*, p. 28 ff.

Reverend Moon and the Challenges of the Modern World

Marcelo Alonso

In order to properly assess Reverend Sun Myung Moon's vision of the world, it is first necessary to make some preliminary considerations.

It is generally recognized that we are living in a dynamic and complex world in which changes are taking place at a rather fast pace. And this applies not only to *physical* changes, such as new roads, buildings and living styles, but also to changes in attitudes as to the recognition and judgment of values, which we might call *cultural* changes. We all share the responsibility of making sure that the world changes in the right direction and that our children and the children of our children inherit a better world. For that it is very important to understand the factors that affect the world's dynamics and the challenges they pose.

One of the key factors responsible for world's dynamics is the explosion in knowledge that has occurred in the last four decades in terms of producing new knowledge and its application to a variety of purposes. This is the phenomenon that is designated as the emergence of *post industrial* societies, of which the United States and Japan are among the leaders; also Korea is rapidly approaching a post industrial status. These knowledge-producing societies have contributed to a deeper understanding of the physical world from the smallest things such as elementary particles, the basic building blocks of matter (electrons, protons, neutrons, quarks, etc.) to the largest structures of the universe, such as clusters of galaxies. The systematic application of new knowledge in turn has resulted in an ever increasing number of new products and processes that not only have changed our life

Dr. Marcelo Alonso

style, but have stimulated in most of us an insatiable desire for material things.

While tremendous amount of wealth has thus been produced and accumulated, unfortunately these riches are not equally accessible to all. Some countries have advanced tremendously in the economic sense while others still remain very poor. Some countries produce excess of food while in others there is hunger and physical misery. Thus, among the several critical challenges that the world faces there is one of particular importance. This challenge is how to make sure that as our knowledge in all disciplines advances and new applications are developed, scientists working together in an interdisciplinary way contribute to the welfare of *all* people in the world and not for the benefit of a few at the expense of many.

A second challenge faced by the modern world is the erosion of values. The avidity for material things in modern technological societies would not by itself be wrong if it were accompanied by a proper recognition of moral and ethical values. Lack of recognition of values weakens the practice of justice, love and charity in those societies and makes them vulnerable to all sorts of human abuses, including crime, drug addiction and corruption.

This problem is compounded by another aspect of scientific and technological progress: a deeper understanding of life phenemena from the physical or structural point of view that tempts us to look at man as a highly sophisticated machine. In this view, man operates according to the physical laws of interaction among the atoms and molecules that constitute the human body without any transcendental element. This extreme position has obviously a profound bearing on the understanding of the meaning of values. Thus the second critical challenge reduces to how, as we learn more about the physical world and about the human body and understand better human behavior, scientists, philosophers and religious leaders can join forces to restore and reinforce in our free societies the proper respect and recognition for the basic human rights and values.

There is a third challenge faced by the world that perhaps is the most important in the long term, but also more difficult to achieve: peace. Peace is an aspiration that all humans expect to enjoy. We can achieve inner peace or peace of mind through personal efforts. Peace in the family is also easy to achieve through mutual tolerance and love. Peace in our neighborhood is possible through mutual respect. But when we come to peace at a national level or at world level the goal seems more elusive.

Why do we not have world peace? We can invoke several explanations all conveying part of the truth, but to me in this modern world of today, the most serious obstacle to world peace has been the emergence of a pseudo-scientific doctrine denominated "dialectic materialism," the foundation of an economic and political doctrine propounded by Marx and Lenin, and carried into practice as a political system in what is nowadays called "communism." Without entering into the analysis of Marxism-Leninism, its interpretation of matter as the objective reality as perceived by our senses, existing outside mind and being the object of cognition, a position which is basically correct, has been carried too far to propound a view of history as an inexorable deterministic process (what is

called "objective historical necessity"). Besides being totally false, this theory of history downgrades the role of humans in the universe and essentially negates values, and ignores the role of technological progress as a factor of unpredictable changes.

Because Marxism-Leninism advocates violent change from "old" to "new" social orders, it has given rise to dogmatic revolutionary systems that have deprived large segments of the world population of their most basic rights. And this deprivation has been done by force and not by people's consent. Unfortunately, due to the ruthlessness with which Marxist-Leninist revolutionaries push their ideas and political systems, more and more countries have fallen under communist rule since the victory of the Bolshevik Revolution in Russia in 1917. As a consequence, we witness today an ideological confrontation between the value oriented democratic open societies and the communist or Marxist-Leninist dictatorial governments tightly controlled by ruling elites that maintain the principle of "violent change" to achieve their goals.

In summary, I consider that three of the most important challenges that we face are: 1) create a more just and fair world as our scientific and technological knowledge increases, 2) make sure that in our advanced technological societies moral and ethical values are properly recognized, and 3) assure peace in the world, for which it is essential to stop and reverse the advance of communism.

II

Many political and religious leaders as well as scholars all over the world have recognized at different times these three challenges. However, in most of the instances the analysis has been done in partial or fragmented ways, and not as an indivisible whole. To my knowledge, only one person has recognized in recent times that these three challenges have to be dealt with in an integrated and unified way, and this person is the Reverend Sun Myung Moon. He is the only person that is expending extraordinary personal efforts to mobilize the academic community and political and religious leaders to analyze and develop a better understanding of these three challenges and explore or find the proper solutions, and he is expending considerable financial resources toward creating the conditions for carrying out these solutions. It is for that reason that I have enthusiastically accepted the invitation to cooperate in Reverend Moon's efforts to achieve these goals. I am pleased to recognize that those invitations carry no strings attached, particularly in terms of the acceptance of his own personal religious views, no matter how respectable they might be. In all cases I have been rewarded with a most fertile and creative atmosphere which has resulted from the total freedom for discussing at the highest intellectual level the issues mentioned above. Next, I will review briefly some of the activities sponsored by Reverend Moon related to the three challenges I have mentioned.

I am pleased to recognize in the first place the International Conference on the Unity of the Sciences (ICUS) as the only interdisciplinary event at which scholars from all over the world gather to consider and examine different problems related to the first two challenges in the context of two major themes: "The unity among the sciences and all fields of knowledge," and "How to place values at the center of science." It is true that many scholars have some doubts about whether there is any relation between the sciences or knowledge and the notion of values, especially moral and ethical values. I concur that to the extent that the scientific activity is strictly concerned with seeking the "truth," the problem of values has no bearing. However, since the scientific truth is not absolute, but is continuously evolving as knowledge increases, scientists continuously confront situations that in some way touch upon the problem of values and that require an interdisplinary effort for their clarification. Let me give some examples:

We know that we all have a marvellous organ called "brain" which is the center of command of our nervous system and the processor of the information received from the external world. But we also know that we have the ability to think, to reason, to have feelings, to exercise judgement, to distinguish between good and evil, etc—functions that constitute what is called the "mind". Obviously the relation between mind and brain is a critical one for deciding upon such important aspects as human behavior, responsibility, free will, and judgement, all of which have value implications. This relation between mind and brain is still an open scientific question that has been examined at great length at ICUS.

Our recent understanding of biomolecules and the role they play in genetics and the life process has permitted to develop a new scientific branch called "bioengineering" by which genetic material can be manipulated to alter the characteristics of some organisms or even to produce new ones. Although bioengineering techniques have not yet been used with humans, in principle they are applicable to humans. And there is no question in my mind that tinkering with human genetic material poses a serious value problem. This is another area of interest for ICUS.

Recent scientific research has provided information about how the universe has evolved since its beginning at what is called the "Big Bang" which it seems occurred approximately 15 billion years ago; its evolution through different stages until the emergence of large structures such as stars and groups of stars called galaxies, about one million years later; the origin of the solar system which is an extremely small group of minor bodies in a corner of our galaxy, which dates from about 5 billion years ago; the emergence of life on Earth, about 3 billion years ago, and finally the appearance of man on Earth as recent as a few million years ago. These scientific discoveries have removed man from being the center-piece of the universe, contrary to the cosmogonies of the traditional religions. Nevertheless, humans are the most delicate and elaborate living entitities, and the more we know about ourselves the more awe we should feel. This evidently requires a revision with great humble-ness of our views of the place of man in the universe, man's purpose, if any, in the cosmos, and a re-examination of the two great metaphysical questions as posed by the Greek writer Nicholas Kazantzakis: where we come from and where we go from here. But this in no way diminishes the role of man in relation to its immediate environment and its moral and ethical responsibilities. In fact, humans are the only living beings concerned with these matters. This evolutionary view of the universe provides a common ground for analysis by scientists, philosophers and theologians, for which ICUS constitutes an adequate forum.

Needless to say, there are many other areas in which science has to be concerned with values, such as the use and preservation of natural resources and the environment, the provision of adequate food and energy for everybody, etc., which have also been discussed in ICUS. The problem of science and values can be summarized in the following statement by Reverend Moon: "Technology (that is, the use of science) is a tool whose value depends upon the purpose for which it is used."

The unity of knowledge poses a different set of problems to be dealt with in ICUS. In the gradual ascent of man, to use Bronowski's terminology, knowledge was acquired empirically and through our sensorial experiences. In this way a great diversity of disciplines or branches of knowledge emerged in the course of time: physics, chemistry, biology, engineering, medicine, psychology, etc. Philosophical thought and religious doctrines evolved in parallel and, except for few instances, with little interaction with the sciences and their applications. This situation is quite unsatisfactory, and in the modern world totally inadmissible, since the universe is one and its analysis must be carried out in a unified way. Bridging the gap between the different physical and life sciences has been possible recently thanks to our unified understanding of matter, which has occurred in the last 50 years or so, but closing the gap between science and philosophy, including religion, is a task that has not been accomplished yet. This is why ICUS is so important, since it provides the opportunity for that kind of discussion.

The very justified concern of Reverend Moon with building a world in which values play a key role has led him to establish in Washington D.C. an independent non-profit research and educational organization called The Washington Institute for Values in Public Policy, which provides analyses of the ethical values underlying public policy issues. The complexity of the contemporary world has resulted in the situation that most policy decisions contain inevitable value judgements. Policy issues of current interest in the United States are, for example, abortion and the value of human life, human rights and U.S. relations with dictatorial governments, nuclear energy and nuclear weapons, and so on. For those reasons The Washington Institute has become a well recognized center for providing analyses, orientation materials, and position papers related to a diversity of policy issues both national and international, on which the U.S. government has to be involved and take positions. I have had the privilege of collaborating in several projects of the Washington Institute. The projects in which I have been involved include two task forces from which books have resulted: *Central America in Crisis* and *The Nuclear Connection.*

As it is well known, the Soviet Union, using Cuba as its base of operations, has initiated a determined effort to impose communism in Central America by giving strong support to the guerrillas in El Salvador and to the Marxist-oriented Sandinista government in Nicaragua. Unfortunately not many people understand what is happening in Central America. *Central America in Crisis* provides a historical, political, economic and sociological analysis of that region and the nature of the violent confrontation going on there, so that people can understand the problems faced by those countries and contribute to their resolution.

The book *The Nuclear Connection* examines an equally important problem: how to increase the use of nuclear power for electricity generation all over the world without increasing at the same time the risk of proliferation of nuclear weapons. There is no question that nuclear weapons must be proscribed from the world. Their mere existence pose a serious risk to every civilization, and no country know this better than Japan. On the other hand, the peaceful use of nuclear energy is absolutely necessary. Oil and coal are two very important resources, but their amount is limited and their use produces considerable pollution. Nuclear energy contributes to reduce the consumption of oil and coal. In particular, the 5 nuclear plants in operation in Korea (with a total capacity of 3,580,000 kW) have reduced the oil imports by 36 million barrels per year, with a yearly savings of more than 500 million US dollars. Japan generates about 16% of its electricity in 32 nuclear plants (with a capacity of 26,000,000 kW) which represents a displacement of 260 million barrels of oil per year or, at the current price of $15 per barrel, a savings of about 4000 million US dollars per year. If people understood better these economics, and realized that using nuclear power does not imply having nuclear weapons, there would be much less opposition to the use of nuclear energy. Hopefully *The Nuclear Connection* contributes to this understanding.

The above two examples can give an

idea of the importance of the value-related issues addressed by The Washington Institute.

I would like now to address briefly the third challenge I have referred to, that is world peace, and to mention some of the activities sponsored by Reverend Moon to meet this challenge. In the first place, Reverend Moon recognizes that it is most important that the obstacles to world peace are clearly understood and solutions sought. This is the purpose of the Professor's World Peace Academy, which holds meetings all over the world on specific issues pertaining to each region or to the world as a whole. I strongly recommend *The International Journal on World Peace,* an excellent quarterly publication of PWPA, that is a forum for the dissemination of critical analyses related to world peace.

Reverend Moon also recognizes that to achieve world peace it is essential to stop and reverse the onslaught of communism as a political system and of Marxism-Leninism as its philosophical or doctrinal base. In fact, one of the most appealing aspects in Reverend Moon is his clear position against communism as a morally unacceptable doctrine and form of government. The recognition of this fact has motivated Reverend Moon to establish another institution called CAUSA to examine in detail Marxism-Leninism from the ideological point of view and offer an alternative of higher social and moral values. I have had the opportunity of participating in several of the seminars organized by CAUSA, which were well attended by distinguished participants with different backgrounds but all equally motivated by the desire to pre-serve democratic values and stem the loss of the Third World to communism.

Two outgrowths of CAUSA are the Association for the Unity of Latin America (AULA) and the International Security Council (ISC). AULA is dedicated to analyze the obstacles that prevent the ideological and economic unity of Latin America in the context of free democratic systems of government. As such,it studies political, legal, economic, social, scientific, educational and cultural problems faced by the Latin American countries with the aim of formulating a policy for the unity of Latin America. Its exofficio members are past presidents elected democratically or who have been instrumental in the transition to democratic systems in their countries. But AULA also involves a number of well recognized politicians and experts in Latin American problems. I have had the opportunity of participating in their discussions of economic, social and scientific issues, and I feel quite encouraged that AULA will play a very important role in promoting a better understanding of the problems of Latin America and in reversing the expansion of communism in that region.

The International Security Council (ISC), also sponsored by CAUSA, is an independent institution whose aim is to provide a responsible and expert voice on international security affairs in a way free from political and diplomatic constraints. The ISC holds conferences and seminars and publishes position papers on matters affecting the security of the international community, such as state-sponsored terrorism and the Soviet threat in the Caribbean Basin. The ISC also publishes a quarterly, *Global Affairs,* which offers a forum for scholarly papers dealing with international security issues. I have participated in several ISC activities; in particular I was moderator in discussions of the nuclear balance and defense space technologies, subjects of great relevance for preserving the world from a nuclear holocaust.

Needless to say, there are many other projects sponsored by Reverend Moon in which I have not been directly involved, such as Paragon House Publishers, *The Washington Times* and *Insight Magazine* which provide the public with balanced information on a regular basis, and several cultural activities, of which the Little Angels School and Performing Art Center in Seoul stands at the top. These projects simply arouse my most profound admiration and respect.

I wish to conclude with some personal remarks. Why, being a nuclear physicist by training and vocation, have I been involved in the activities I have described above? If as a professional I were to act only in the narrow field of my specialization, I should be involved only in the study of the structure of matter, quantum theory and nuclear energy. As a citizen, however, I recognize that I have responsibilities that go beyond my direct professional interest. Fortunately, during my days as Director of Science and Technology of the Orga-

nization of American States, I became interested in the problems of the developing world and how science and technology could help in their solution. I quickly realized that I could not extricate science and technology from political, economic and educational issues, and that value judgements were involved in many of these issues, a point ignored by many people. I also was able to appreciate the difficulties of promoting cooperation among the countries of the region, in spite of their ethnic and cultural similarities, because a diversity of political and economic problems. And above all, I became aware of the threat of communism, that was taking advantage of the sufferings and limitations of the underprivileged sectors of the population in Latin America, and under which I had suffered in my own native country, Cuba, which I left early in 1960 shortly after the establishment of the current communist regime.

Thus when I was offered the opportunity of dealing with all those issues as a private citizen, without the hindrances of governmental or institutional limitations, I could do nothing but enthusiastically accept. So far, I do not regret my decision, just the opposite. I am proud of it.

FOUR

ACTIVITIES TO STRENGTHEN DEMOCRATIC INSTITUTIONS

The Necessity of Moral Regeneration: The Contribution of Reverend Sun Myung Moon

Morton A. Kaplan

The world is facing parlous times. This is particularly obvious in Korea, a divided country facing a dangerous enemy in the North. The armed forces of North Korea are concentrated for a lightning strike toward Seoul. Although the North's forces are larger and better equipped than the forces of South Korea, my Korean students instead see the Southern forces as stronger. They deny that Kim Il Sung or Kim Jong Il had anything to do with the bombings in Burma or the invasion tunnels. That was all done by lower ranking officials, they say, against the wishes of the top officials. These are the same kinds of comments that Ignazio Silone, the famous Italian novelist recorded in his novel of fascist Italy *Bread and Wine,* in which all evils are attributed to underlings against the wishes of Mussolini. In both cases, of course, this is sheer fantasy, although a psychologist would recognize the mechanism of denial.

In Korea itself the radical students hold secret study sessions in which they convince themselves of what I regard as intellectual nonsense. Under American influence Korean industry has been oriented toward the export market, they say. The simple fact is that Korea possessed neither the skills nor the domestic market that could undergird many elements of industry. The former could be acquired over time—but only by participating in the world market—and the latter is unchangeable for the foreseeable future. Thus, the only way in which Korea could purchase what it could not produce was by exporting things that other countries would buy. And by doing this, South Korea was able to find both skills and markets for the production of automobiles, electronic equipment, and other technological products

Dr. Morton A. Kaplan
in Tokyo, Japan

that the domestic Korean market could never have justified and in the absence of which it would have remained a poor and backward country.

The economists tell us that there is no such thing as a free lunch. There is a price to Korean development: vulnerability to world market conditions. The United States is also more vulnerable to world conditions than when only 10% of its trade was foreign. Some irresponsible or ignorant American politicians who are banking upon the economic illiteracy of the American public are pushing for restrictions on imports. But the price would be ridiculously high. To save a $30,000 job in the automotive industry in the United states, for instance, would cost the American public $80,000 per year and several jobs elsewhere in the economy. Similarly, an autarchic economic policy would have kept the South Korean economy in a sad state. The decision not to do so, in any event, was made by President Park and the bright technicians he employed, not by the United States.

These radical students also claim that Korean prosperity was purchased by the low wages paid to labor. That is an extremely misleading claim. South Korea was able to expand its trade in part because of low comparative labor costs. But these wages were low only compared to advanced countries, where there was more human capital and far better logistics. The wages were higher than would have been possible in Korea in the absence of foreign trade. And as the human capital of South Korea has advanced, the industrialization and wage levels have also advanced. Korea is no longer one of the world's poorest countries, and its workers can afford a standard of living that would have appeared miraculous in 1960. With so many Korean professors teaching classes and signing manifestos, I wonder why these simple facts of life are not being taught to Korean students.

It is true that South Korea is not a democracy as Americans understand the concept. And I certainly do not celebrate this fact. The government can exercise excessive control over industry and its use of police powers permits a mild authoritarianism that impedes the opposition. But there are opposition parties, honest elections, the promise of a peaceful transition of authority that seems believable, and the statement of the ruling party that it accepts the premises of democracy.

There seems to be a clash between the Confucian culture of traditional Korea that permeates the army and the Western-style culture that characterizes the highly-educated elite. But a minor segment of this educated elite seems to be a captive of the ideological spirit that began to captivate Europe and Japan in the 1930's and the United States in the 1960's. Most seem to have forgotten that Mussolini started as a left-wing socialist, that Hitler called his party the National Socialist German Workers' Party. Both Communism and fascism were revolutionary movements directed against bourgeois, capitalist democracy. If one reads early Bolshevik pamphlets, the propaganda of Hitler and Mussolini, the letters of the Spanish falangists or of the members of the Japanese Black Dragon Society, or of the American Students for a Democratic Society, one cannot but be struck by the similarity of themes and images: themes and images that recur in the activities of radical Korean and Japanese students.

The themes include attacks on capi-talist calculation and prudence and an emphasis on heroism and self-sacrifice. In their proper place, I might even sympathize with these latter values. But they also involve a collective subordination and a lack of respect for individuality and self-direction. I am no supporter of a completely instrumental culture in which the only question is: What is in it for me? Aristotle spoke of the golden mean, that is, of balance between values that when pushed too far become vices. And I think that there is no doubt that these radical student activities have become corrupt and dangerous and destructive vices. These "self-study" sessions are really indoctrination sessions—in which the will to believe not merely subordinates but entirely derogates the reflective self that alone can be the source of reasonable moral or political behavior.

These dangerous tendencies are also reasserting themselves in Western Europe. The reaction to Chernobyl illustrates this. Gorbachev was in fact correct when he spoke of Western exaggerations, although, given the Soviet exaggerations on Three Mile Island, where no injuries occurred, he was in a poor position to complain. In a plant that was constructed so poorly, even by Soviet standards, and about which there were complaints in the official Soviet literature before the accident, there were only a few deaths and the long-term incidence of cancer in the particle path will be increased only by a small fraction of 1%.

I am not suggesting complacency. Had I been in the particle path I would have been worried and furious. And I particularly support the long-standing suggestion of Edward Teller that we design and build inherently accident-free plants, now a quite feasible project. But the anti-nuclear hysteria that Chernobyl generated made manifest a failure of nerve and a type of political hysteria that is dangerous for free institutions.

This dry rot of the moral nerve attends our discussions of most issues today. Let us take the example of South Africa. I hope there is a universal agreement that apartheid is evil. But from this alone no conclusion follows with respect to particular policies. For it does not follow that bringing down the present South African government will produce a better situation. Most governments in the world are tyrannies. And some are tyrannies of a majority population over a minority population, whether distinguished by tribe, race or religion. It is difficult to understand why a minority tyranny is necessarily worse than a majority tyranny. There is no magic in majorities. The democratic belief in majority rule can work only within a framework of consensus on basic values, for only then is it better to lose and keep the system than to revolt, if that is possible, and capture it. If we wish to overcome the evil of apartheid and are convinced that it is possible, we ought to be concerned about what will replace it.

The task before the world community is not to turn South Africa over to so-called majoritarian rule, which may produce only a new destructive dictatorship that removes civil rights from all but a small handful of rulers while wrecking the economy, but to achieve a system of at least minimal justice in which the rights of all ethnic groups are protected. This will not be an easy task, for in addition to the enormous grievances the blacks understandably have, the rural black population has no knowledge of or experience with modern political systems.

The world is afflicted with another deadly disease: the decline in civic virtue. Today large numbers of young people ask only what is in it for them. There has been an enormous decline in patriotism and altruism. This is not merely the product of capitalism as some claim, for the same tendencies can be found in even exaggerated guise in the socialist and Communist nations. There corruption, self-advancement, and contempt for those not included in the elite has reached an unprecedented nadir.

Even worse, the ordinary citizen is regarded merely as an object of state or Party power in those countries. In Soviet Russia, for instance, those who dissent are placed in insane asylums and treated with drugs, evidently on the theory that no sane person would reject utopia. But we are on the verge of scientific discoveries that will enable us to change genetic structure and to use chemical and electronic means to coerce not merely what people do but what they believe. Such devices in the hands of governments unconstrained by morality and convinced that only thus can public order be maintained may create a situation in which humanity, in the sense that any decent or God-fearing person would understand it, may cease to exist. Although many fundamentalists believe in Armageddon, T.S. Eliot may have been closer to the truth when he suggested that the world may end not with a bang but with a whimper.

However, the scourge of nuclear war cannot entirely be excluded. The risk of war lies not in an intention on the part of the Soviet Union to start such a war, or even in an intention to seek world control, but in the economic failure of the Soviet system. The costs of armaments weigh heavily on the United States also, but the failed Soviet economic system buys armaments at immense costs to its own people. The costs of this process are so high that, alone among so-called advanced nations, the Soviet Union faces decreasing longevity and substantially increasing infant mortality. Absenteeism, sabotage in the workplace, drunkenism, and illness characterize the Soviet system, except for an elite with special privileges and access to special stores.

This weakness inherent in the Soviet system produces internal dissent that under some circumstances may seem threatening to the regime. If lack of unity and dissent occur in the West, the Soviet Union may see a crisis in Western Europe—a crisis that by mistaken calculation leads to war rather than the desired peaceful acceptance by the West of Soviet demands—as an opportunity to smother dissent by manufacturing an external threat.

The factors that may create an opportunity to do this already have been alluded to. The Greens in Germany represent an extreme version of the decadent beliefs and political values to be found in Western Europe, but more moderate versions are not uncharacteristic. The Labor Party in Britain and the Social Democrats in Germany have strong factions supportive of unilateral disarmament. But even in the so-called conservative parties, large elements of their supporters are driven by counterproductive fear.

Any sane person would be fearful of terrorism or nuclear war. But when fear becomes a governing emotion, as it is for a majority in Britain, Germany, and Italy, then it produces behavior that increases rather than decreases the risks. Those who are too fearful to act become natural targets of the very risks they seek to avoid.

President Reagan was roundly criticized for his military action against Libya. Although it was possible that it might have produced a momentary upsurge in terrorism, it in fact did not. Yet few in Europe have been willing to credit the relative success of this extremely modest action. There are convincing reports that Colonel Ghadafy is quite worried, that some members of the Libyan junta are now restraining him, and that President Assad in Syria has become more circumspect in his support of terrorism.

The primary response to this parlous state of world affairs must be that of moral regeneration. Moral people are not so self-centered that the defective social practices of which I spoke earlier are acceptable to them. Nor do they lack self-confidence to such a great degree that they crumble in the face of danger.

In this respect, the activities of Reverend Moon and the Unification Church are of great assistance through their demonstration of faith and their self-assurance that withstands prejudiced attacks from hostile organizations and governments. Genuinely inspirational figures are rare in world history, and the example of Reverend Moon undoubtedly restores hope to many people in an enormous number of countries in every continent on this globe.

If I attempted merely to enumerate the religious, charitable, and educational activities sponsored by Reverend Moon and the Unification Church, I would have to stand here for several hours.

Reverend Moon is responsible for the Victory Over Communism movement and CAUSA, which stand as bulwarks against Communism in many countries but particularly in Asia and Latin America. He founded *The Washington Times* which plays an important role in Washington D.C. in assuring accurate presentation of important world news.

Reverend Moon is also the sponsor of the world-wide Professors World Peace Academy with chapters in more than eighty countries. PWPA sponsors many different educational projects in many different countries in its endeavor to make the world a better place for all and to improve the prospects for peace. While opposed to Communism, this organization works to improve relations with Communist countries such as the Soviet Union and China in the interests of world peace. It recently sponsored a major international congress on Soviet Russia and is planning to hold a similar congress on China as part of its educational efforts. It sponsors a journal *International Journal on World Peace* that explores how differences among countries and peoples can be accommodated in the interests of peace and with the Washington Times Corporation it publishes *The World and I,* a 700-page

monthly journal that will become an encyclopedia of the contemporary world.

Reverend Moon also sponsors the International Conference on the Unity of the Sciences, which annually brings together scholars from more than 100 countries to advance the state of the individual sciences. These conferences have been graced by the presence of leading Nobelists. They produced important books which are published by Paragon House Publishers, which under the moral guidance of Reverend Moon is becoming rapidly a major international publishing house.

That one man, Reverend Moon, has accomplished all this in little more than 30 years is a continuing miracle. On several occasions I have recommended against projects as too difficult to achieve only to discover that Reverend Moon's faith and his church can move mountains and perhaps one day will serve as an Archimedian lever to move the world.

To those of you closely associated with Reverend Moon, you have been touched with greatness. To those who know him, you have been graced. To those who know of him, you have much to learn. To those who have contributed to his successes, you have reason for great satisfaction.

Reaffirming American Constitutional Principles

Albert P. Blaustein

Introduction

America is getting ready for a great holiday. It is the celebration of the 200th anniversary of the constitution of the United States—the world's first national constitution. It is a time for the reaffirmation of the principles which underlie this constitution; it is a time to reexamine the fundamental ideas and ideals of Americanism; and it is a time of rededication to the struggle for freedom and democracy.

An important figure in this reaffirmation, reexamination and rededication is the Reverend Sun Myung Moon. And I want to talk about his role from the perspective of a professor of constitutional law. For Reverend Moon has taken leadership in the continuing struggle for religious freedom—that freedom of conscience which many consider the basis of all freedoms. And he has likewise assumed a leading role in the struggle against communism—the foremost enemy of democracy and freedom.

Reverend Moon calls the United States "the miracle of modern history." He believes that "God played a prime role in American history and this He wants America to know." The Reverend Moon preaches "Godism." This Godism is idealism, utopianism. It sets forth ideals to which we should all aspire. And in reaching for those ideals we can create on this earth a Kingdom of God or Heaven. Such a Kingdom depends upon a good constitution (in fact, many good constitutions) to which we must adhere and whose precepts we must practice. Interestingly, he has likened the three branches of government: executive, legislative and judicial, to the heart, lungs and stomach of human beings: they must work together in an orderly and harmonized manner.

So much for the underlying philosophy. But what has been done—specifically? How has Reverend Moon contributed to the reaffirmation of constitutional and democratic principles?

What is a Religion?
We know that the Unification Movement began approximaly a quarter century ago in Korea as one of the many revivalist Christian religions which flourished in that nation following World War II. But was it a religion? Was it a church? This was important to the leader of that movement because it meant so much to his credibility in preaching for freedom of religion in the United States. Those who denied that it was a religion called it a cult. Those in Europe who denied it was a religion called it a sect. The courts in America ruled otherwise.

It was in two cases in 1982 that the courts first made strong statements affirming the validity of the church:

> ...the Unification Church, by any historical analogy, philosophical analysis, or judicial precedent... must be regarded as a bona fide religion. *Unification Church vs. Immigration and Naturalization Service*, 547 Fed. Supp. 623, 628 (D.D.C. 1982)

The New York State Court of Appeals (the highest court in this most important state), in a unanimous decision concerning the right of the Unification Church to a property tax exemption on religious grounds, said this:

> [We] conclude that on the record before us, as a matter of law, the primary purpose of the Church (much of whose doctrine, dogmas and teachings and a significant part of whose

activities are recognized as religious) is religious. *Holy Spirit Association vs. Tax Commission*, 55 N.Y. 2d 512,528 (1982).

The courts of Michigan used similar language in 1984. So did the Federal appellate court in New York in 1985 and the California appellate court in 1986. So this point is settled for good.

The Moon Trial and Its Aftermath
The story of the trial and punishment of Reverend Moon on charges of what the American government called "tax evasion" are well known. I will not go into the details of that trial and the eventual conviction, but in brief: monies brought into the United States for the work of the Unification Church were, as is common practice, given to Reverend Moon and deposited in bank accounts in his name. Because these were church monies and churches are tax exempt, no taxes were paid on the interest which these monies earned in the banks. But the tax people said that since the funds were in the name of an individual that individual would have to pay an income tax. This led to the imprisonment of Reverend Moon. He has since served his term and is again a free man.

I was privileged to play a small role in that case as the author of one of the briefs submitted to the United States Supreme Court urging it to hear the case on appeal. Significantly, my fee was paid not by the Unification Church but by the Freemen Institute, an organization dominated by the Mormon Church which works for freedom of religion. That was by no means the only church organization which joined in asking the Supreme Court to review the case. There were many—for this became a cause celebre which marshalled many religious groups to act in concert. All religions and religious groups were being threatened by the decision in the Moon trial.

There were also briefs by the American Coalition of Unregistered Churches and The Religious Freedom International, plus the American Association of Christian Schools, the Catholic League for Religious and Civil Rights, the Church of Jesus Christ of the Latter-Day Saints, the Coalition for Religious Freedom, and the National Council of the Churches of Christ in the U.S.A., together with the Presbyterian Church (U.S.A.), the American Baptist Churches in the U.S.A., the African Methodist Episcopal Church, the National Association of Evangelicals and the Christian Legal Society.

But it was not only religious groups which banded together in what they all realized was a part of the continuing struggle for religious liberty. Because constitutional issues were involved, there were also briefs by the American Civil Liberties Union, the New York Civil Liberties Union and the National Emergency Civil Liberties Committee.

The end of the trial did not end the activities of these groups; quite the contrary. That is the main story. The trial of Reverend Moon was a catalyst and an inspiration in bringing religious groups together and keeping them together in the ever-continuing struggle for religious liberty. This "grouping"—this unification—has resulted in many meetings and conferences, in the publication of many books and pamphlets, in the bringing of many law cases, in tremendous publicity and in intensive teaching on the subject of religious liberty.

The matter of religious liberty is a constitutional issue which also has

Dr. Blaustein sightseeing near Nakasaki, Japan

stirred the secular community. It may be *the* constitutional issue. America not only pioneered in constitution-writing but was the pioneer in establishing a bill of rights; one of whose rights was freedom of religion. But in modern constitutional thinking, inspired in part by Reverend Moon, such freedom is not just "one of those rights." Freedom of religion is freedom of conscience. It is freedom to think as one chooses to think. It is freedom from state-imposed thought. Thus many consider it *the* fundamental human right and say that without this freedom all the others are without meaning.

The Struggle Against Communism

Affirmative support of human rights, freedom and democracy necessarily means opposition to communism. While almost all Americans oppose communism, unfortunately, very few ever do something about it. The Reverend Moon takes the threat of communism seriously, and he has spearheaded a large segment of opposition to communism in the United States. He has established, among other things, News World Communications which has spawned many publications, all of them strongly anti-communist. Flagship of this enterprise is the *Washington Times,* now one of the most-quoted newspapers in the United States. The entire organization has been put under the supervision of Dr. Bo Hi Pak whose exploits as a soldier are so well known to all Koreans. But he has wisely given free rein to the editors. *The Washington Times* and its companion *New York City Tribune* (and their counterpart in the Spanish language) publish the leading anti-communist editorialists and columnists, as well as giving a side of the struggle against

communism all too often missing in the American press. Having been privileged in having my own writings published in the *Washington Times,* I can testify as to its impartiality.

I would like to tell you about one organization which is the vanguard of the anti-communist struggle: CAUSA. It started as a Latin American organization concerned with the spread of Cuban communist activities in the Western Hemisphere, but now it is worldwide in scope. In its many publications and during its many meetings it has explained the nature of the world communist movement and educated its audiences as to the dangers with which we are being threatened.

But more than this, it has offered an alternative to communism. And here I want to use some of the language of Dr. Bo Hi Pak, president of CAUSA International, who, with Messrs. Tom Ward, William Lay and Antonio Betancourt, has lectured and written tirelessly on this subject.

The CAUSA movement, explains Dr. Pak, "is an ideological movement." CAUSA considers communism to be an ideology. And he emphasizes: "Communism can only be defeated by a superior ideology or worldview. We offer... a world view based on philosophical and scientific reasoning."

I have been privileged to speak at CAUSA meetings on the topic of constitutionalism. I believe in the importance of constitutions in obtaining and maintaining freedom. I take the view that "human rights violations are symptoms; the disease is the absence of constitutionalism." CAUSA makes a similar analogy.

The famous anti-communist activist Dr. Fred Schwartz has made this statement: "I am against communism because I am against war, dictatorship, monopoly, slavery, facism, fratricide, cannibalism, imperialism, atheism, materialism, spiritual infanticide, and idolatry. Communism advocates and practices all of these." Now to Dr. Pak's observation: "Dr. Schwartz is correct... They are all symptoms of applied Marxism. But like any disease, there must be a cause, or an original virus which has produced these symptoms. For that reason, we need to ask, what is the virus or core evil of communism? Unless we discover this, we cannot prescribe a cure. That means we can never stop communism." But what is that core evil?

Answer: *"It is communism's absolute denial of the existence of God."*

The struggle is to make people understand the need for "Godism"—not the viewpoint of a particular religion or denomination but the realization of a God-centered worldview. This is the message of CAUSA and of Reverend Moon. It is also the message of this constitutionalist. For, as I noted earlier, the basic human right is freedom of conscience, freedom to believe and think as one wants. Only such free people can be sovereign in their own right. Only such free people can promulgate their own constitution.

The Never-Ending Pursuit of Liberty Equality and Fraternity

Nicholas N. Kittrie

It is with great pleasure that I am addressing the academic communities in Korea and Japan. I believe that in assessing the human condition worldwide and in looking forward to tomorrow's world, the central stage cannot be left to the professional planners and politicians alone. There are major issues involving philosophy, values, concepts of man, and concepts of the universe which must be taken into account in the planning for and the shaping of a better world. The task of bringing these important issues into proper consideration, in your countries and in mine, must be undertaken and carried out by those committed less to the exigences and pragmatics of the moment and more to the long-term aspirations of man and the transcendental values of religion. The members of the academic communities, teachers, professors, and philosophers, therefore, must join ranks in making sure that their input is strongly felt not only in the world of ideas, but also in the worldly pursuit of better global politics, economics, and social reforms.

Coming to Korea and Japan during the month of July, I continue being aware of the event which to us is most central for July—the celebration of the American Revolution. Before I deal more directly with the contemporary missions that I believe we must agree upon and jointly carry into effect, I wish to share with you some of the lessons to be derived from America's own historical struggle for liberty.

July 4th of this year marked the two hundred and tenth anniversary of the American Declaration of Independence. The fathers of the Declaration were amongst the most politically distinguished, economically well-to-do, and socially prominent community leaders in the English colonies. Nonetheless, they did not see their task as merely that of bringing about political reform or evolutionary change. With great zeal and with little hesitation they draped their efforts with a radical tag: revolution.

Many modern-day radicals instinctively scoff at this revolutionary claim. These radicals, mostly in the left, but also on the right, will concede that America's uprising was a war of national liberation. For a *revolution,* however, they will point to the French example (with the guillotining of Louis XVI, the redoing of the calendar, and the imposition of a reign of terror) or the Bolshevik prototype (founded on state endorsement of atheism and the institution of a dictatorship in the alleged name of the proletariat). This fashionable contemporary denial of America's revolutionary origins, seemingly confirmed by America's present-day willingness to be cast in the role of prime guardian of the status quo, is seriously detrimental to the American quest for world leadership. The truth of the matter is that America's nature and outlook were, and continue to be, revolutionary.

What was so sudden, drastic, comprehensive and far-reaching in the American struggle for independence, one may ask, to rightfully endow this nation with the mantle of revolution? With the passage of more than two centuries it is not surprising that we have lost track of the true significance of the American revolution. Even our more patriotic high school history teachers do not seem to appreciate how different the American revolution of 1776 has made today's world, both at home and abroad. Many political principles now taken for granted, practically throughout the

world, were first promulgated by the American revolution. The American revolution comprehensively denied the political wisdom of the time, and replaced the old principles with new ones. The American revolution denied the right of empire, that some nations should be allowed to rule other people as their colonies; denied that kings and princes had a divine right to lord over the people; and denied that government is the primary source and guardian of the peoples' rights. Instead, the American revolution articulated, for this country and the world, the following new and radical principles: the recognition of the innate or "natural" right of the people to "life, liberty and the pursuit of happiness"; the realization that undue governmental intervention might hinder the full realization of these rights by the people; and the recognition of the people's right to change their government, by either lawful political means or by popular uprising, whenever those in power cease to conscientiously discharge their sacred trust on the people's behalf.

Yet despite this early and persisting commitment, in words and in deeds, to the principles of the Declaration of Independence, America as a nation slowly seemed to be losing both some of the convictions and the rhetoric of its revolutionary mission.

A central factor to produce a retrenchment in America's revolutionary stance was the advancement of Marxist ideology in the world marketplaces of politics. It was Karl Marx, and Lenin and Stalin after him, who claimed the ownership of "the true revolution." The Bolshevik revolution was indeed a drastic and a frightening experience. Resorting to the tactics of the reign of terror utilized in post-revolutionary France, the Soviets starved scores of millions, executed millions, and imprisoned hundreds of thousands of real, suspected, or potential counter-revolutionaries. In a Russian society barely coming out of the throes of medieval feudalism, they proclaimed the failure of capitalism and turned the economy back, in the name of revolutionary change, into a totalitarian, state-owned and managed feudal estate. Neither did the unwavering atheism of the Soviet leadership (harping back to the French revolutionary dogmas) and their materialistic doctrines (springing from the dialectical philosophies of Marx and Engel), leave much breathing space for the peoples' religious, political, and economic liberty.

Dr. Nicholas N. Kittrie

But instead of branding Lenin and Stalin as false Messiahs and the Soviet revolution as a false dogma, the United States relinquished the revolutionary arena to the pseudo-revolutionaries. It is their red flag, as a consequence, that is currently being hurled out by the disgruntled, disenfranchised and unprivileged. America thus seems to have withdrawn from the revolutionary contest—we have come to be viewed as the haves, the care-nots, the defenders of the establishment and the preservers of things the way they have been.

In this beginning of the third century following the American revolution it is incumbent upon us, therefore, as the foremost economic and military power in the world, to also take stock of our ideological arsenal. The time has come, once more, to reassert our revolutionary stance and commitment. Our position and goal have not changed from those articulated in the Declaration of Independence. We believe in private property and in free enterprise as means for bringing about the greatest amount of economic well-being for the greatest number of people. We believe that enlightened self-interest and political as well as economic competition are essential ingredients for change and progress. We believe that life, liberty and the pursuit of happiness cannot be dictated or granted from above, but must be constantly nourished by those seeking their benefits.

Coming before you today, it is my desire not only to talk about liberty, the major goal of the two hundred year-old American Revolution, but about two more current central needs of the nations and peoples of the world: equality and fraternity. I am not talking merely about legal and political equality. I am talking about the kind of equality of opportunity in the economic, social and communal realms that would allow people to rise from the depths of deprivation and lack of opportunity to attain a more autonomous role for themselves, their families, children and communities. Man is said to be created in the image of God, and it is imperative that that image be revered, enhanced and guarded wherever it is found.

I wish further to add to our previous agenda of liberty and equality also the indispensable ingredient of fraternity. Fraternity means supplying the individual the proper environment, the proper setting, the proper government, the proper communal institutions for man and woman not to feel alone, unattended, alienated. Fraternity means an enhancement of the family institutions, school facilities, children's playgrounds, workers'associations, and religious collaboration.

I wish to take notice that these three goals of liberty, equality and fraternity

were indeed pronounced nearly two hundred years ago by the French Revolution. But soon enough these goals were betrayed by the leaders of the French rebellion, who turned instead to a Reign of Terror and eventual fratricide of unequalled dimensions.

As we are here today I urge that we rededicate our efforts to a peaceful, cooperative, collaborative and conciliatory, loving and dedicated pursuit of true liberty, equality and fraternity throughout the communities of nations and throughout all corners of the world.

I think it is telling that these series of meetings were being called for and arranged by the Unification Movement. Indeed the agenda of these meetings fits very comfortably with the ongoing efforts, during the past forty years, of Reverend Moon, who set out to sensitize not only his own adherents in Korea, Japan, the United States and elsewhere, but also members of other religions and denominations, political movements and persuasions of the urgent need for thinking man to take stock of his presence and his future.

I wish here today to pay tribute to the many creative, innovative, and at times, indeed, revolutionary undertakings of Reverend Moon and the Unification Movement. As some scholars of the Old Testament have emphasized—you best know a man, you best know a leader, and you best know even a nation, not by their words but by their deeds. Reverend Moon's deeds are the highest and best testimony to the role he has played in the past forty years—in bringing together scholars from all over the world to work for the unity of sciences, for recognizing the role of mass media and the need to imbue media with an awareness of values, with the constant effort to improve social and economic conditions throughout the world by supporting and instituting programs of training and self-help.

It is my pleasure to be here today on behalf of Professors World Peace Academy. PWPA is another precious stone in the crown of Reverend Moon's achievements. It is through this organization that academics from all over the world, regardless of their own particular disciplines and even their country's hostilities, are able to cast differences aside for a creative effort for the betterment of the world and for individual conciliation. It is with great amount of satisfaction and pride that I have participated in the work of PWPA. I invite all academics here in Korea and Japan, and throughout the world to take part in this constructive, selfless and forward-looking organization.

Let me conclude with just a few additional words. Our sponsorship is dedicated and everlasting: the ancient biblical commitment (shared by Jews, Christians and Moslems) as enhanced by the wisdom and the benevolence of the Far East from which Reverend Moon, himself, has come. Our ranks are easy to ascertain: PWPA will join forces with all kindred organizations for the pursuit of a better world community. Our mission is simple: the greater and more vigorous pursuit of liberty, equality and fraternity.

FIVE

PEACE, JUSTICE AND GLOBAL COOPERATION

The Quest for Peace: A Vew from Anthropology

Raphael Patai

On a stone wall facing the United Nations complex in New York are engraved in golden letters the words:

> They shall beat their swords into ploughshares,
> And their spears into pruning hooks,
> Nation shall not lift up sword against nation,
> Neither shall they learn war any more (Isaiah 2:4).

These eternal words, uttered by the great Hebrew prophet Isaiah in the eighth century B.C., embody a dream of world peace which today, almost three millennia later, is still far from being realized. Conflict-proneness has remained the greatest scourge of mankind, even though the founders, seers, and teachers of all the major religions— Judaism, Christianity, Islam, Hinduism, Buddhism, Jainism, Confucianism, Taoism, and Shintoism—have uttered condemnations of war and preachments of the imperative of brotherhood, unity, and peace.

The sad historical fact is that through-
out the five or six millennia that have passed since man has left behind his first written records he has always lacked peace and unity, the two fundamental ingredients without which human happiness and fulfillment cannot be attained.

Clearly, what is needed today is a global peace effort based, not on a narrowly conceived religious particularism, but on a broad anthropological understanding of the diversities of human cultures, and on the recognition that despite the incontrovertible validity of each culture for its own carriers, all cultures possess common all-human elements and values. It is in the identification and pointing up of these commonalities comprised in all local cultural configurations that the best hope lies for developing a common cultural basis for world peace. This is the approach that the Professors World Peace Academy, founded by the Rev. Moon, must utilize in its work. Let me explain briefly how I envisage this being capable of accomplishment.

The various complexes which make up the totality of each culture can be arranged into a scale ranging from those which lend themselves most readily to harmony among all human groups, or in which, already at this point in time, there is a measure of agreement, down to those complexes in which at present agreement is minimal or even non-existent, and in which it will be most difficult, albeit certainly not impossible, to work out an understanding. The most important of these complexes, listed in order of ascending difficulty they can be expected to present are as follows:

1. Technology
2. Medical and Health Services
3. Scientific Research
4. International Commerce
5. Foreign Aid
6. Communications
7. Literacy and Education
8. The World of Art
9. Political System
10. The Realm of Religion

Let me now say a few words about each of the ten culture complexes enumerated, always keeping in mind the extent to which it serves or can serve as a unifying, or divisive, factor in world relations.

1. We begin with *technology* which, by its very nature, spreads most easily across national, continental, and cultural boundaries. Today technology, which

not so many years ago was the privilege of Western Europe and the United States, has established itself in all parts of the world and is utilized by all countries irrespective of political or religious ideologies. The technical aspect of culture is the one in which international exchange is the easiest, the most general, and the most pervasive. How little technology is culture-bound can best be seen in those countries into which modern technology has penetrated only recently, and several of which, notably Japan and Korea, have in fact overtaken technologically the Western world in some areas. Technology is an enormously influential culture complex which, once it strikes roots, tends to transform life as a whole and recast it in a mold in which global similarities overshadow traditional local cultural features. As far as technology is concerned, it is no exaggeration to say that the industrial centers of all countries all around the world constitute today one global village. The potential of this global technological commonality for the promotion of world peace has so far not been sufficiently explored.

2. *Medicine and health services* are closely related to technology, and their character is likewise predominantly international. The prevention and curing of disease and the alleviation of physical pain are universal human concerns, and no political system, whether democratic, totalitarian, or based on fundamentalist religious doctrines, does knowingly prevent the application of medical knowledge and practices, irrespective of the country in which they have originated, and however negative its views of the political doctrines dominant in that country. Natural and man-made disasters which require large-scale

medical aid have for many decades now brought about international cooperation, despite all political antagonisms. The 1986 atomic catastrophe in Chernobyl, in whose wake Soviet Russia received medical and technological aid from the western democracies, supplied a fine example of the ability of medicine to forge a link between rivals. Medical cooperation is a channel of great peace potential.

3. *Scientific research,* although connected by many strands to medical research, is not as readily shared across international and ideological boundaries. Both the communist countries, in which research in physics, chemistry, and other sciences is a state-controlled and state-sponsored activity, and the western democracies, in which such research is more often than not left to private enterprise, guard jealously the results attained in their laboratories and experimental stations. Moreover, rivalry in this area exists not only between the east and the west. Countries allied and joined by a common political ideology also compete with each other for prestige, leadership, and recognition, as exemplified, e.g., by the Nobel Prize. Still, the scientists in each of the major fields of research form international communities with close contacts and cooperation, and the journals in which they publish their research results are major global channels of communication. In the further development of a global scientific commonality lies one of the great hopes of mankind for harmony, peace, and unity.

4. In *international commerce* the cooperative and competitive factors are about evenly balanced, with cooperation having perhaps a slight edge. Enlightened commercial self-interest recognizes that

Dr. Raphael Patai confering with Prof. K. K.Chang in Seoul, Korea

trans-national cooperation, expressed e.g. in concessions and voluntary self-limitation, better serves the national purpose in trade than ruthless, cut-throat competition. A healthy economic situation in any country is one in which exports and imports are, roughly, balanced, and while a large trade surplus may appear desirable from a short-range point-of-view, in the long run a serious trade deficit in one major segment of the globe inevitably causes business to experience difficulties in other parts as well. International economic interdependence is today a fact which few countries in the world can afford to disregard. This development augurs well for world peace, for the greater their international economic interdependence the less likely are countries to resort to its armed disruption.

5. *Foreign aid* is a parallel development which, since World War II, has reached formerly unimaginable dimensions. Today, in all the economically well-off countries it is taken for granted that they have to give aid to the less developed or developing countries, including economic and technical assistance, relief from the catastrophic consequences of natural disasters, food to alleviate hunger, and efforts to help poor countries to become self-supporting and improve their living standards. Although the expenditure of developed countries on foreign aid is woefully small compared to their outlays on armament, still many billions of dollars are annually transferred in foreign aid from rich to poor countries, 95% of it coming from the United States, Canada, Japan, Australia, and the non-communist countries of Europe. Today, no nation can any longer consider itself in isolation from the well-being of other nations even in the most remote corners of the earth.

6. *Communications* are a relatively new culture complex, and one whose importance has greatly increased in recent years, especially due to the computer revolution. Communications are a very specific ingredient in culture inasmuch as, in contrast to all the other culture complexes, it has no message of its own, but serves their dissemination. By the 1980's communications have become an indispensable part of the cultures of all the technologically advanced countries. Communications have gained great importance in international relations, and as such have begun to serve the preservation of peace between antagonistic and mutually suspicious powers, as exemplified, e.g., by the Washington-Moscow hot-line. The rapidly expanding network of communication satellites makes it possible today for an event occurring, or a politically significant statement made, in practically any country to be known almost instantly all over the world.

7. That global *literacy and education* is an indispensable prerequisite of global peace may not be a self-evident proposition, but a moment's consideration of the closed, inward-directed, xenophobic nature of illiterate societies will make us see the connection. Hence one of the ways of working for world peace is to spread literacy in the remaining illiterate areas of the world.

We must, of course, be aware of the magnitude of the task. Literacy can be spread only by introducing general and compulsory elementary education, and this, in turn, can be done only at the cost of considerable social upheavals which the governments of developing countries are often loath to trigger.

Which, again, forces upon us the conclusion that what is needed in those world areas where illiteracy is still rampant is a far-reaching social reform.

8. *The world of art* to which we come now, is an aspect of culture in which no obvious common denominators, such as those of literacy and education, exist. Quite to the contrary: art has remained to this day one of the values most intrinsically intertwined with, and expressive of, local traditional cultures in every corner of the earth. And yet, at the same time, art is also international and transcends national or political boundaries. A cultured person, whether he is the product of a Western, an Indian, or an East Asian culture, enjoys not only the arts of his own native land, but also art originating from entirely different cultural milieus.

Hence, art must be regarded as one of the most promising avenues leading to international understanding, and ultimately to world peace and unity. Art can bring about a global harmony in human affairs within which the variety and diversity of the creative human spirit can be sustained. Art, while preserving its individuality in every culture, can be the living bridge between the most diverse countries, simply because the artistically awake individual is receptive of even the most different art styles, and senses the underlying common human values which characterize true art in all cultures.

9. With *political systems* we come to the first of the two most difficult areas as far as international understanding is concerned. The differences between the free democracies, the various types of communist totalitarian systems, and the rightist dictatorships seem irreconcilable, and perhaps so they are at present.

Most pronounced are the differences between the two super-powers, the United States of America and the Soviet Union, each the leader of a large bloc of nations.

Yet the relations between the two super-powers are far from being totally antagonistic. There are considerable areas of agreement between them. They both agree, e.g., that whatever their differences, they must be settled, not by force of arms, but by peaceful means, negotiation, persuasion, and compromise. Scientific, cultural, and artistic exchange between them has by now a history of several decades. Economic and commercial relations are gradually expanding between the democratic West and the communist East. The struggle for arms control, limitations, and reduction continues despite periodic setbacks.

I do not want to sound too optimistic about the possibility of reaching a true understanding between the two opposing political systems. At the present time the gap between them is too wide to be easily bridged. Even if two halves of one and the same nation belong to the two opposing systems, the antagonisms between them are bitter, fueled, among other factors, by the envy the communist half, with its stagnating economy, feels for its brethren who live under a free market system and enjoy economic progress. The two Germanies and the two Koreas exemplify this situation. Nor can any amount of sophistry explain away the unceasing attempts of thousands to leave the communist countries, and to seek, despite walls, watchtowers, and armed guards, to escape into the free world, while no corresponding movement exists in the oopposite direction. Phenomena such as these make one realize that an understanding between the communist and the democratic countries will require prodigious efforts.

What, in view of the position of the communist world, can we do in order to draw it into the orbit of such peace-oriented efforts as those of the PWPA? Some options, while limited, do exist. PWPA could try to set up chapters in the less restrictive communist countries. A small delegation of member professors, speaking the native languages of the communist countries in question, could be sent there to explain what it is the PWPA is trying to do. Meetings could be organized in non-aligned countries where professors from both the communist countries and the western democracies could meet on neutral ground and exchange ideas. Peace, after all, is such an all-human ideal that participation in discussions of how to work for it must, sooner or later, be countenanced even in those countries which have their own orthodox Marxist view of the brotherhood of man.

10. Lastly we come to *the realm of religion*. Here we tread on extremely sensitive ground. Religious commitments to traditional values affect human attitudes more deeply than do political convictions.

The major religions of the modern world fall into two overall categories which can conveniently be termed *theistic* and *non-theistic* respectively. The three great monotheistic religions of the Middle East and the West—Judaism, Christianity, and Islam—are the foremost theistic religions and the dominant faiths of about one half of mankind. Common to all theistic religions is a pronounced religio-centrism, expressed most poignantly in the conviction that one's own religion is the one and only

true one, and that all the other faiths are erroneous and hence deprecable.

The great non-theistic religions of South-east and East Asia, notably Hinduism, Buddhism, Jainism, Confucianism, and Taoism, lack the element of self-assurance and certainty that each is the exclusive possessor of the only truth. There is a wonderful parable which illustrates the nontheistic view of man's quest for truth. The truth, so it goes, dwells hidden atop a very high and very steep mountain. A group of seekers sets out from the foot of the mountain in search of the truth, but the mountain is too steep to climb up directly, so they start circling it, gradually rising in a spiral fashion as they go round and round. Halfway up the mountain they encounter another party which circles the mountain in the opposite direction. When they meet, both parties tend to believe that the others go in the wrong direction. But the wise will know that, whether they circle the mountain to the right or to the left, both seek and are on the way towards the same truth. Because of this insight, not reached by the traditional creedal theistic faiths, the eastern non-theistic religions are tolerant of one another.

What then are the chances of achieving a common religious denominator for mankind as a whole? It would, first of all, appear that this will be less difficult to work out in East Asia where the dominant religions are not only non-theistic and non-creedal, but also non-aggressive, non-proselytizing, and tolerant. In fact, in these world areas, in which lives about half of the human race, the merger and combination of religions has been going on for centuries. In contrast to the interreligious exclusiveness of the West, it has repeatedly been noted in East Asia that individual families are often composed of Buddhists, Confucians, and Taoists, and that even one and the same individual often follows two or all three of these religions. In a society in which this is the basic religious attitude it seems inevitable that the recent intensification of communications should before long lead to the emergence of a unified religious world view which, in turn, can serve as one of the main pillars of the future edifice of world peace.

In South-East and East Asia, communist China, Vietnam, and North Korea constitute a difficult problem from the point-of-view of religious harmony. The official communist doctrine is anti-religious and atheistic—we must not confuse the atheistic position with the non-theistic!—and one must face the fact that world communism is as much an obstacle to global religious harmony as it is to global understanding in the other aspects of the endeavor for world peace and unity.

The achievement of religious harmony in the non-communist West is also beset with difficulties. In those sectors of the Western populations which are more or less indifferent to religion the search for religious harmony is likely to encounter a belittling attitude. As for the religiously committed sectors, they can be expected to have an a priori antagonistic reaction to any search for religious harmony, because they will be inclined to regard any such attempt as an infringement of the claim each particular religion has staked out to the exclusive possession of religious truth. Hence any work for religious harmony in the West will have to be conducted with utter caution and circumspection and will have to concentrate, to begin with, on locating and identifying the common features among the theistic religions, such as the belief in the existence of one single creator God, which is the most basic tenet, the one cornerstone upon which are built all of the many and varied edifices of the Western religions. On that basis it might be possible to initiate dialogues among them, and then continue toward a broader search for harmony and toward that religious unity which in turn may prove to be one of the most promising avenues towards global peace.

The final lesson we can learn from the foregoing discussion of the various aspects of world peace is that while peace is indivisible, in the sense that there cannot be complete peace in any part of the world unless there is peace everywhere on earth, there are many roads that lead to peace, and it is the great challenge of an organization devoted to peace such as the PWPA to explore all of them simultaneously, tirelessly, and assiduously.

Reverend Moon and the "New" Pacific Community

Cromwell Crawford

There is much talk today of the 21st century as a "Pacific Century." Norman Macrea of *The Economist* observes that the economic capital of the world is no longer in the region of the Atlantic but of the Pacific. Futurist Herman Kahn forecasts that the Pacific will become the "new Mediterranean" in which the future of mankind will take shape. Kiyoshi Kojima, eminent Japanese economist, sees the present threats to world peace and order overcome by "the creation of a new and dynamic world development center" within the Pacific Basin, because of its "great overall potential."[1] Secretary of State George Shultz expresses similar sentiments in a recent address. He says:

> To understand the future, you must understand the Pacific... In economic development, in the growth of free institutions and in growing global influence, the Pacific is increasingly where the action is. As important as it was a few years ago, it is even more important today. And it will be even more so tomorrow.[2]

Factors which are cited in the literature to support these optimistic prognostications are many and varied.

Geographically, the Pacific is the largest ocean in the world, covering one-third of the globe. Its tides sweep across five continents—North and South America, Asia, Australia and Antarctica.

Demographically (1975 figures), the population of the Pacific Basin is a towering one billion, 835 million, as compared to the 259 million of Western Europe. Fully two-thirds of the human race live in Asia and around the Pacific Ocean.

In terms of resources, eight of twelve most vital strategic materials come from this region. These waters contain the

Dr. Cromwell Crawford

largest fish stocks in the world—a bountiful source of protein.

Economically, East Asia is growing faster than Europe. From 1973 to 1980, South Korea's world trade exports had grown by 663% in seven years, and Japan's, by 205%. During the same period, West Germany's trade grew by only 160%.[3] Looking ahead, in July 1986, *Time* magazine brought together 19 distinguished economists from 13 countries, who issued a comprehensive assessment of the non-Communist world's prospects. Their prediction for 1987 is that while the growth of the U.S. GNP will remain in a trough of 2%, and that of Europe at a stronger 3.5%, East Asian nations will come out, as usual, as the top performers. They expect Japan to come roaring out of its doldrums, boosting growth from 1.8% this year to 5.7% in 1987. South Korea's economy is expected to surge to a "spectacular" 9% in 1986 before cooling ever so slightly to 8%.[4] Exceptions to this growth will be the cases of Malaysia and Indonesia that are dependent on commodity exports—rubber and oil, respectively.

Thus, the overall picture of the Pacific Basin is that of "a new and dynamic world development center." This is why leading scholars are of the opinion that the time is ripe for promoting the idea of "The 'New' Pacific Community." Robert Oxnam, President of the Asiatic Society, says:

> Having recently returned from a short trip to Korea and Japan, I find myself more than ever impressed by both the dynamism and the increasing integration of the East Asian region. Indeed even the term "Pacific" seems to be taking on new connotations these days. When I grew up, the "Pacific" referred to an ocean

or to a theatre of war. Today more and more people are seeing the growth of a "Pacific community" of nations tied by diplomacy, trade, strategic interests and cultural and educational exchanges.[5]

Where does Reverend Sun Myung Moon stand in this picture of the New Pacific Community?

First we take a glimpse of this man. It is more than a little propitious that this figure should be stepping up on the world stage at a time and in a place which is destined to give shape to the 21st Century. Further, as a son of "the land of the morning calm," he possesses an insider's knowledge of the abilities and aspirations of his fellow Asians. Here, the stumbling block for the West becomes the stepping-stone for the East. Most importantly, Reverend Moon is more than a preacher of the word; he is a doer of deeds. Judged by the multiple humanitarian projects he has launched upon these waters and elsewhere, Reverend Moon is a veritable one-man United Nations!

In the current jargon of theology, the term which best describes this man and his mission is *praxis*. Praxis means the combining of doing with thinking. Reverend Moon is not content to think about the world but wants to change it. His quest is global and elemental. He is not "anti-Communist"; he is pro-life. He sees life as having direction. Just as the waves are pulled by the heavens and move toward distant shores, he feels the need for purposeful action through the hominization of science for a prosperous and peaceful world. In his words:

> Up to now, although science in its quest for truth has investigated immediate causes of particular phenomena, it has not taken up the search for motives or reasons for existence as a whole. Thus the final challenge that science confronts is this question of the ultimate reason for existence. The unexplored problem in the question, "What is the true nature of material?" is that of the reason for its existence, and again, the untouched problem in the question, "What is the true nature of life?" is the very reason for life itself.
>
> I propose that, in clarifying reasons, one must first admit purpose, and before admitting purpose one must first recognize the will that made the purpose, namely, the cosmic and universal will that transcends all things. When you call this cosmic will "God" then the initial step in clarifying unsolved questions is first to apprehend God's purpose of creation, and second to perceive that along with the physical or chemical factors in all material and life phenomena there exists a causal motive directing each thing towards a certain purpose.[6]

The next question deals with the nature of the principles by which human purpose is realized.

The first principle proceeding from Reverend Moon's thought that is applicable to the advancement of the Pacific Community is interdependence. This concern is clearly spelled out in the statement describing the "World Professors' Lecture Tour Through Korea." It specifies as its goal "peaceful co-existence and co-prosperity based on the sense of the community... freed from partisan feeling and egoism."

Interdependence is indeed the first step toward progress in today's world. Editor George Chaplin states: "With growing trade between countries the Pacific Basin interdependence becomes a fact of life."[7] Interdependence produces prosperity. In the early period between 1965 and 1976, not counting bi-lateral US-Canada trade, commerce between trading partners of the Pacific made a seven-fold leap from $15 billion to $105 billion! In the following decade, 1970-78, US commerce in this region multiplied four-fold to $76.6 billion, making US Pacific trade larger than its Atlantic trade. The same has been true for other countries, and all the indications are that this intra-regional trade will only increase.

However, interdependence not only produces prosperity but tension. When nations band together there is inevitably a certain amount of attrition to the control that they can exercise upon their destinies. There is therefore the tendency to take individual actions in order to protect or promote their private interests, especially in matters of food and energy. As a result, in the words of a US government report: "The nations of the region have noticeably failed to manage the reality of economic interdependence." This is the chief cause of friction between the United States and Japan, because Japan has failed to act upon its promise to open up its market to US imports.

Reverend Moon's economic philosophy makes it clear that within an interdependent system, selfish policies may achieve short-run profits, but in the end, devices such as protectionism are not only costly to the market system, but even more costly to the country that has pursued parochial interests.

A second principle essential for the community is multilateral thinking. This follows from Reverend Moon's constant espousal of dialogue as the only rational means of understanding one another. To appreciate this mode of communication one needs only to recall the disastrous consequences of the unilateral and bilateral thinking which turned the Pacific into the most brutal theatre of war.

The best example of the progressive aspect of multilateral thinking is ASEAN (Association of Southeast Asian Nations), comprising the Philippines, Indonesia, Malaysia, Thailand, Singapore and Brunei. Oxnam points out that in the past decade, "ASEAN has become one of the most dynamic regional associations in the world." They have developed "important economic, strategic and political links and have emerged as a growing force in regional and global affairs. In the process ASEAN has become a key counterweight to the Vietnamese domination of Indochina and thus has disproved the once-popular 'domino theory.' "[8] The fact is, that Communism is only attractive to nations that are poor, divided, fearful, lacking confidence, and not communicating with their neighbors; when nations are prosperous, Communism loses its appeal. Even so, this whole area is wary of Communism. "Asian nations are apprehensive that the United States not tie itself too closely to China. Arms aid would be of particular concern."[9]

The third principle of Reverend Moon, so vital for the well-being of the Pacific community, is pluralism. What multilateral thinking is to politics, pluralism is to religion and culture.

The question of religion emerges when one considers the building of a Pacific community on the order of the European Economic Community (EEC). All parties are agreed on the need for such an instituion to raise the standards of living for all Asians, but the problems connected with this scheme are equally clear. Unlike the unified European community, Asians are split along lines of technological sophistication, history, race, and religion.

Addressing the last problem pertaining to religion, Everett Kleinjans, former President of the East-West Center in Honolulu, observes that whereas the European Economic Community draws on religious principles which, nothwithstanding internal feuds, are solidly within the frame-work of Judeo-Christian and Greco-Roman beliefs; the Pacific community is splintered into many faiths, ranging all the way from Animism to Zen. He comments:

> Such differences will constantly intrude into the process of communication and cause misunderstanding. In fact, another challenge in building the Pacific Community is to determine which ideas and values will predominate, a process which occurs in any pluralistic grouping of people.[10]

Reverend Moon is rightly averse to the predominance of the ideas and values of any single religious group. Just as multilateral thinking is opposed to the attempt of any single country to try to impose its own grand design upon the sovereignty of others, the pluralistic thinking of Reverend Moon is opposed to all forms of religious imperialism and religious dictatorship. Instead, he invites all religions to combine their special insights to achieve what none can achieve by itself, namely, the solving of moral and social crisis confronting humanity.

His pluralism goes even further. A staunch believer in the unity of all knowledge, Reverend Moon brings scientists and humanists together in international conferences to strive toward an ecumenism that will create a peaceful and harmonious global culture. In all of this his method is not eclectic but synthetic, respecting individual differences so long as they are spiritually uplifting and socially productive, and at the same time utilizing communal proximity to learn from one another and to create a peaceful and harmonious global culture.

I have personally participated in numerous conferences sponsored by Reverend Moon and have grown as a scholar by the opportunities of having dialogue with Asians from around the Pacific rim who are Hindus, Muslims, Christians, Confucians, Shintoists and Buddhists. The dialogue is also uniquely expanded by crossing over conventional disciplinary lines. Our purpose is not to convert anyone, but to expand our fund of knowledge in a socially uplifting way. Nor are these conferences a ploy to win over scholars to the Unificationist point of view, or to win academic respectability. Theologically, I sharply dissent from a majority of Unificationist doctrines, in the same way as I differ from the doctrinal positions of other churches; but whereas these other denominations would treat me as an outsider, the Unificationists are hospitable to dissent and seem to be developing an uncanny ability to roll with the punches.

To summarize: we have heard from economists, futurists and statesmen that the 21st Century belongs to the Pacific Community. But the prior question is: to what does the Pacific Community belong? By now we know that there is no particular value in growth for growth's sake. It is the quality of life that matters most. Three essential values which belong to the heart of Reverend Moon's mission are endorsed today by Pacific leaders as the building blocks of their new community—interdependence, multilateral thinking and pluralism. When these values are distilled, they spell prosperity through peace, and that is what the word 'Pacific' is all about.

Notes

1. Quoted in, George Chaplin, "Pacific Basin: Dynamic Economic Frontier," *Honolulu Sunday Star Bulletin and Advertiser,* August 10, 1980. Many of the statistics found in this article are taken from this source.

2. Quoted in Robert B. Oxnam, "The 'New' Pacific Community," *Asia,* Nov/Dec 1984, p. 3.

3. "Asia's Importance to the U.S.," *Honolulu Star Bulletin,* Dec. 2, 1980, p. A-10.

4. "A New Age of Capitalism," *Time,* July 28, 1986.

5. Oxnam, *op. cit.,* p. 3.

6. Rev. Sun Myung Moon, "Founder's Address," Proceedings of the thirteenth International Conference on the Unity of the Sciences, September 2-5, Washington D.C.

7. Chaplin, *op. cit.*

8. Oxam, *op. cit.,* p. 3.

9. A. A. Smyser, "Focusing on the Pacific," *Honolulu Star Bulletin,* Dec. 2, 1980, editorial page.

10. Quoted in George Chaplin, "Pacific Basin: A Mix of Rich and Poor," *Honolulu Advertiser,* Aug. 11, 1980.

A Vision
of a Just World

Elliott P. Skinner

As an anthropologist interested in diplomacy, I have been quite impressed with one of the primary goals of the Reverend Sun Myung Moon and of his movement, which is to create a better life for all of the peoples of this increasingly crowded planet. When he addressed the assembled delegates at the plenary session of the tenth International Conference on the Unity of the Sciences here in Seoul, Korea on November 9, 1981, the Reverend Moon declared:

> There are many confrontations and struggles in human society today. Confrontations exist between what might be called the upper and lower classes of races, nations and societies, but the most serious problem of all is the confrontation between the upper and lower classes formed by the difference between wealth and poverty.
>
> The human population in the northern hemisphere centers mostly on the white people and is estimated at about 800 million. This groups may be considered the upper class of peoples of the world. On the other hand, in China, India and other Asian nations, there are 3 billion people who form a middle class of peoples. Finally, centering on the black and brown people, the 500 million of Africa, Central and South America, and Oceania form an economically poor, or lower class of peoples. The difference in economic wealth presents itself in today's world as a most serious problem, and is repeatedly dealt with as the so-called North-South problem by a number of international organizations, including the United Nations.
>
> The most probable way of solving this problem is to unite these upper and lower classes through the Asians who are between the white Euro-American societies and the black African societies. All the important issues of the twentieth century today must be solved on a worldwide scale.[1]

What especially attracted my attention was that the Founder of the International Cultural Foundation had uttered almost the same words about the state of the world as did a great Afro-American, Dr. William Edward Burghardt DuBois, close to a century before. Emerging from Harvard University in 1896, and viewing the world with a visionary perspective that the Reverend Moon would have appreciated, the young DuBois declared:

> The problem of the twentieth century is the problem of the color-line,—the relation of the darker to the lighter races of men, in Asia and Africa, in America, and the islands of the sea.[2]

DuBois lived long enough to witness World War II and the decolonization of much of the world. He ended his days in the Republic of Ghana, one of the first states in Africa, to achieve independence from Europe.

Unfortunately, the departure of the Captains and the Kings from their conquered realms did not bring about the end of that chasm between the rich and the poor that the Reverend Moon talks about. In fact, given the growing indebtness that exist in the world, the question is whether this gap can ever be bridged. Happily, there are leaders such as the Reverend Moon who not only recognize this problem, but are willing to permit persons such as me to join him and his hardworking (sometimes too hardworking) staff to help deal with the problem of the "haves" and the "havenots."

As a member of the Board of Trustees of the Washington Institute for Values in Public Policy, it has been my great privilege to work with other dedicated men and women to commission projects, conduct research, and to examine public policy issues, in the hope of being better able to serve mankind. The Reverend Moon has been wise enough to encourage Mr. Neil Salonen, Director of the Institute, to gather about him persons from diverse political interests and professional backgrounds to help in the work of an organization that is increasingly being seen as one of the more important think-tanks in Washington D.C. After all, the motto of the Washington Institute is taken from the writings of Thomas Jefferson: "We are not afraid to follow truth wherever it may lead, nor to tolerate any error so long as reason is left free to combat it."

As the President of the Washington Institute, Dr. Richard Rubenstein will tell you, we are a busy lot. My particular task is to deal with Africa, where I served as a former diplomat and, incidentally, worked very closely with some of your Korean ambassadors. As you all know, there are problems in South Africa, the last place on the continent of my ancestors to be ruled by persons of European origin. I suggested to my colleagues at the Washington Institute that the United States' policy of "Constructive Engagement" was not working. They listened to my arguments, debated them, and they permitted me to organize a conference with the theme: "Beyond Constructive Engagement." The suggestions which came out of that conference will hopefully encourage the United States to help South Africa to become a democratic society with majority rule, but with protection for the white minority. The contemporary global system can tolerate no less.

My second task at the Washington Institute is, based upon my expertise as an anthropologist, to remind my colleagues of the conviction of the Reverend Moon, that "All the important issues of the twentieth century today must be solved on a worldwide scale." You must understand that we anthropologists take the entire world as our frame of reference, or as we Americans sometimes say, "as our oyster." In fact, my specialty is the rise of a global civilization. I am attempting to understand the meaning to all mankind of MacDonald's "double archs" and Hilton Hotels all over the world, and of people all over the world driving Toyotas and wearing clothes made here in Korea.

The Reverend Moon did suggest that Asia can play the role of mediating between the North and the South, or between the First World and the Third World. Well, Asia is already playing that role, and playing it well. Quietly, but effectively, Asians are diffusing to all of mankind the technological wonders of the modern world. As an American, I wonder whether Asians are not becoming too efficient, but as a person of African descent, I can only welcome the evidence that what Asians can do today, the Africans can do tomorrow.

Notes

1. Sun Myung Moon, *Science and Absolute Values*, (New York: ICF, 1982) pp. 97-98
2. W.E. Burghardt DuBois, *The Souls of Black Folk*, (Nashville, Tenn.: Fisk University Press, 1979) p. 13.

One World Under God

Ricardo C. Galang

The title of this paper is borrowed from one of the speeches of Rev. Moon. It sounds ambitious and unrealistic; in fact it is. Some skeptics may even say, "One world is visionary. It is impossible." Those who say so forget that God works in strange ways. Nothing is impossible for Him: miracles happened in the past, and they are happening now.

With the Unification Movement as conceived by Reverend Moon, those of us involved in it have made some steps toward one ideal world. The steps may be small, but we know that the longest journey begins with one step. It is said in Oriental philosophy that if one succeeds in beginning a job, he has already finished half of it.

A Bird's Eye View of the World

Time limitations for this presentation do not allow us to look at our world more closely. But the highlights stand out in a panoramic view; namely:

1. We see conflicts everywhere: There are ideological conflicts, e.g. totalitarianism vs. democracy, economic warfare between nations, religious conflict, racial discrimination, etc. And people go to war because of those conflicts: Iran vs. Iraq; Contras in Nicaragua vs. Sandinistas; Catholics in Ireland vs. the Protestants; whites vs. blacks in South Africa; Christians vs. Muslims in the Philippines.

The cost of wars in human lives and material is tremendous: e.g., 3 million Koreans, both North and South during the Korean War in 1950; more than 58,000 Americans during the war in Vietnam; one and a half million Filipinos during the Second World War. As to property: three-fourths or more of Hiroshima on August 6, 1945 was devastated by one bomb, with 90,000 casualties; and the greater portion of Nagasaki was obliterated by another bomb three days later.

2. Destruction of material things affect the lives of people. However, what has been destroyed by man's undoing may be repaired or replaced; but the destruction of man's faith can not easily be repaired.

Thus one other highlight in an over-all view of the world, as a result of various conflicts, is *man's loss of goodwill*, not to mention *loss of trust in humanity.* Human feelings, when hurt, are expensive and sometimes beyond reconciliation.

We all know that wars start in the hearts of man. Anyone who would try to reconcile conflicting convictions needs to understand some basic psychological roots that may be imbedded in man's thoughts. In many segments of human society we find:

More grabbing than giving.

More selfishness than generosity.

More suspicion than trust.

More racial discrimination than neighborliness.

More religious intolerance than ecumenism.

More hatred than love.

More self-centeredness than God-centeredness.

Psychological Roots of Conflict

When you look more deeply into these deviations of human behavior, you discover some possible explanations; for example:

Man's desire for material wealth is rather strong. Since money can buy everything except real happiness, it becomes the end-all of life.

Man's selfishness is rooted in his effort to satisfy his desire to accummulate wealth. Of course we all know the price we have to pay for being what Americans call "filthy rich": a rich man may lose his soul. What profiteth a man to gain the whole world if he loses his soul—this Biblical wisdom is as valid now as it was two thousand years ago.

Man's separation from God, the victory of Evil over Good—this is perhaps the most significant psychological basis of man's behavior. We all know that when man separated from God, his troubles started.

Previous Attempts to Unite the World

The most well-known attempts to unite the world are the League of Nations and the United Nations. The League of Nations was born after the First World War in 1918. President Wilson thought the League would prevent wars; but much to his frustration, the United States Congress did not even approve the League. Wilson died broken-hearted. Twenty three years later another war broke out.

After World War II, the United Nations was born. That most glamorous and most expensive debate club in modern times has failed to eradicate poverty, violations of human rights, drug addiction, and rising rate of abortion. The UN does not have enough force, except moral force, to stop any wars. We in 1986 are no nearer to lasting peace than we were in 1945 when the UN charter was signed. Those of us who witnessed the signing ceremony had moist eyes, praying that man should not go to war again against a brother human being. NATO and The Warsaw Pact perhaps have been deterrents to war; but they are but alliances on either side of a vaster conflict.

Feasible Approaches to One World Under God

What, then, could be some feasible approaches to one world under God? The following may sound too simple to be misinterpreted, but they are given for what they are worth.

First, change the individual. Changes among nations start with the individual. The principal agents of individual character formation are the home, the church, and the community. A good individual might raise a good family, good families may mean a good nation; and good nations may mean a good world.

Dr. Ricardo Galang
in Kofu, Japan

Second, solidify families, many of which are disintegrating. Today, we witness an increasing number of broken homes and divorces: one out of two marriages fail in some states in the American Union.

Third, fight racial discrimination. A person's skin color is not his fault. For under the skin—white or black or yellow or brown—the color of man's blood is the same: red. The so-called blue blood in Boston—where I lived as a student—is only figurative speech.

Fourth, declare war against religious intolerance. Rev. Moon's concept of ecumenism is a binding force. The interfaith activities that Rev. Moon encourages are a bright lining at the edge of dark clouds that hover above the heads of men. At this very moment, we have in the Philippines about 90 young men and women—most of them college students, who render free service to poor communities in that country, building a school house, constructing a bridge to connect a Muslim community with its neighbor, a Christian community, and drilling artesian wells to provide potable water. These young people come from

34 countries: some Christians, some Muslims, some Buddhists, some Sikhs, and others Taoists. And they work together, eat at the same table, pray in their own ways. The Religious Youth Service, as they are called, is a classic example of tolerance, brotherhood, and co-existence. The RYS is unification in action.

Conclusion

I am not aware of any other movement that operates on a world-wide basis comparable to the Unification Movement. The Unification Movement is the only global non-divisive effort to establish universal brotherhood as a foundation for lasting world peace. A one world under God is possible only when a man is a true brother of another regardless of color and creed.

No one of us may live long enough to see a one world under God, but we have the satisfaction of knowing that we have made and are making our individual and collective contributions, no matter how simple, to create an ideal one world. Our best may not be good enough, but at least we can say we are doing our best. Rev. Moon's examples of persistence are our guides.

SIX

THE CHALLENGE AND THREAT OF COMMUNISM TO WORLD PEACE

The Situation of the World and the Unification Movement

Richard L. Rubenstein

It is a great honor for me to return to your country which is fated to play so crucial a role in world history in our times.

As a result of its momentous development, the Republic of Korea is becoming one of the world's most important industrial and technological powers. Regretably, Korea's economic "miracle" has not been accompanied by a heightened measure of national security. Were it not for the presence of American troops, it is very likely that the people of Korea would by now have been engulfed in a civil war far bloodier than that which overtook this peninsula thirty-five years ago. The economic success of South Korea is a perpetual affront to communist ideology. Not only is the Republic of Korea one of the world's most successful capitalist nations, it is also the country with the highest proportion of Christians in all of the Asian mainland. If the communists cannot meet this double challenge by communist performance, the northern regime would not hesitate to defeat it militarily if it could.

Unfortunately, the United States has not always proven a wholly steadfast partner. For example, when President Carter entertained the possibility of withdrawing American troops from Korea, it was obvious to informed observers that the President had a limited understanding of the communist challenge and of the strategic importance of the Republic of Korea to the non-communist world. Fortunately, Carter came to understand something of the dangers of communist aggression before American troops were actually withdrawn. Nevertheless, even though American troops remain in Korea, economic progress of South Korea remains

Dr. Richard Rubenstein
in Tokyo, Japan

a perpetually endangered progress. Koreans can never take it for granted that future American leaders will always understand the challenge of communism as does President Reagan.

There are many aspects of Reverend Moon's work about which I could speak on this occasion, but none are as important as his efforts to counter the threat of communism both for his own nation and the world. As we have seen, the Republic of Korea cannot hope to meet the challenge of communism solely with its own resources. The battle to stem the tide of communism in Korea must be fought in Washington, Tokyo and throughout the major centers of the non-communist world. No son of Korea has done more to meet the communist challenge on a world-wide scale than Reverend Moon. Moreover, as Reverend Moon understands, we are engaged in a battle of ideas and of the spirit at least as much as in a contest of relative military strength. As such, the struggle must be waged first and foremost among those who are the world's decision-makers and opinion-makers.

Let me give you a few of the many examples of the ways in which Reverend Moon is meeting the challenge of Marxism among decision-makers and opinion-makers in the West. It is my privilege to serve as the President of the Washington Institute for Values in Public Policy, founded by Reverend Moon in the city of Washington. The Washington Institute is a research institution whose purpose is to engage the very best available authorities to analyze important political issues concerning which there is significant public debate and to make their findings available to American political leaders. Among the issues explored by authorities affiliated with the Institute have been American policy in Central America, American policy in the Philippines, the future of NATO, the viability of nuclear energy for peaceful purposes, American policy towards Africa, American policy towards Asia, and many more domestic and foreign-policy questions. Our findings have been made public through books, printed monographs and occasional papers. Unlike some Asian countries, such as Japan, where real public policy is made by the bureaucracy rather than elected politicians, in the United States public policy is largely made by elected officials such as the President and the members of Congress. Since elected officials must be responsive to public opinion to remain in office, American elected officials are extremely sensitive to informed public discussion of political issues. That is why their staffs constantly turn to the many public-policy research institutions— "think tanks"—in Washington in order to understand the issues.

In the four years since Reverend Moon founded the Washington Institute, it has been recognized as one of Washington's most notable "think tanks." Indeed, it was so described in an article in the January 1986 issue of *The Atlantic Monthly*. That article, entitled "Ideas Move Men," described how important Washington's "think tanks" have been for the formation of American policy. Indeed, if there has been a shift in American opinion away from a naive attitude toward communism and national defense, much of the credit has been due to "think tanks" like the Washington Institute. Its publications, conferences, and seminars have attracted a very wide audience of public officials and opinion-makers. As you

would expect from an institution founded by Reverend Moon, the research and publications of the Institute are the work of some of the leading scholars and experts from all over the world.

Another notable contribution made by Reverend Moon to the formation of informed public opinion in Washington has been the *Washington Times*. Washington had only one newspaper until Reverend Moon started the *Times*. When the paper was first announced, many people mocked the idea. They said that nobody would take seriously a newspaper published by a Korean religious leader who had been treated so harshly in the American press. Of course, those of us who knew Reverend Moon understood that any project that he decided upon was destined not only to succeed but to be of the highest quality. Today, even his enemies acknowledge that the *Washington Times* is one of America's leading newspapers. The President of the United States has said that the *Times* is his favorite newspaper.

There are literally hundreds of other projects all over the world which Reverend Moon has founded as expressions of his belief in the unity of all religions and all humanity under God. It should be obvious that, by his activities and his leadership, Reverend Moon is refuting Marxism in the most practical way possible. For Marx religion was an opiate, consoling an oppressed class with hopes of a better world to make up for the miseries of their this-worldly condition. Marx did not understand the energizing power of religious faith as does Reverend Moon. Ironically, today it is Marxism that has become the opiate of religionless intellectuals, using the promise of a Marxist version of a better world to come as its bait to secure allegiance in the present. By contrast, there is nothing of the opiate in Reverend Moon's faith or the faith he has instilled in his followers. On the contrary, it is his faith and his capacity to inspire that has enabled him, his followers and scholars, scientists and men of good will who work with him throughout the world to do so much in so short a time.

The Significance of Reverend Moon in the Fight Against Utopian Ideologies

Thomas Molnar

I trust I may be allowed to consider the Reverend Moon's action in the past decade or so under an angle that has hardly been noted. Having travelled much in the world during the last three decades, the primary object of my observation has been the cause of fighting leftist totalitarian regimes and their ideologies. The latter, even when not coagulated into a regime's policies, have had the same deleterious effect: the corruption of minds and morals. In the devastated landscape which is the consequence of what I like to call "utopian" ideologies, rife with false conceptions of human nature and the human condition, all the natural reactions of men are seen through a distorting lens, and are therefore condemned, discredited, ridiculed.

Drug addiction, for example, seems merely a medical problem, but it is in reality a problem created by utopian ideologies which believe that by smashing man's rational and moral defenses, and thus his judgment of good and evil, a *new man* will be created. This new man will be beyond good and evil, and beyond rationality. With only his animal reactions guiding him, he will form perfect communities with his similarly conditioned fellows. He will then to such an extent indulge in emotions, enthusiasms, sex, and hazy view of his environment, that he may then be reduced to a robot, a mechanism, and thus manipulated by his masters. So, from whichever angle you corrupt a human being, by demolishing his natural reactions or regimenting him for evil causes, the result will be the same: loss of the human essence which is what we call the *soul* stamped by God's image.

Now why is this utopian ideology not suitably attacked and dismantled by the saner majority of the intellectual and academic world? I see the main cause of this inefficiency or even paralysis in the fact that utopian ideologues for the past century or so have succeeded in discrediting and caricaturizing man's natural defenses, which I would simply identify as attachment to religion and nation. The French philosopher, Etienne Gilson, wrote about modern scientists and thinkers that they would rather accept the thesis that the universe is the product of chance, than to postulate the existence of a creative intelligence behind the phenomena: God. These scientists are not even tolerant enough to give the two hypotheses an equal chance.

The same thing happens when we observe the modern western discredit cast on the *nation*—the focus of man's primary loyalty, this time not according to the spirit, but according to space, time, language, tradition, custom, and basic identification and orientation. While the idea of the nation is ridiculed, the utopian ideologues look for new, imaginary and artificial roots: a social class, a manipulated group such as "youth", the international proletariat, a political party, or a cultural fashion conveniently advertised as man's this-worldly fulfillment. People are not really drawn to these ideological constructs— the anti-God or anti-nation—by a genuine attraction and mature judgment, but rather through a process which softens their better convictions and appeals to the weaker part of their character.

Strangely, however, the guiding signals are rare on the road which leads modern man to intellectual and moral corruption. Few are the leaders who dare confront fashion—the biggest force in a democratic age—and even fewer

those who present the natural alternative, mankind's oldest loyalties. I have found that most philosophers and so-called opinion-leaders, tough persons in speech and behavior, have a little boy's fear of what the ideological fashion-makers and propagandists will say. The first charges against them will be prejudice, ignorance, reactionary intentions, power-hunger. If the confessor of old loyalties: God, nation, tested institutions, parents, etc. still holds on firmly, the campaign against him will grow, insults and insinuations will be hurled at him, he will be morally stoned. Very few can stand up to such orchestrated pressure; the majority withdraws demoralized, leaving the just-gathered followers dazed, confused, and ultimately cynical. They might never be recruited again for the cause of rationality and the good.

The foregoing brief analysis, based on observation in many lands and all continents, on this and that side of the totalitarian curtain, in the West and in the third world—has led me to a number of conclusions. Granted that the *leader* is firm in his moral understanding and values, and granted also that he possesses qualities which attract people to the fundamental loyalties we just spoke about, what he too often lacks is *courage* to persist in his design, and an *organizational genius* which makes his followers feel that they belong to a unit of loyalty. I have also found that courage and effective organization are qualities much more often found among the corrupters than among their prospective victims. When I say "organization", I mean of course work done according to modern methods; and when I say "courage", I mean the unembarrassed use of these methods, no longer for the cause of utopian ideologues, but for that of their adversaries.

Many hypotheses could be advanced why the *left* proves to be more effective than the *right*. Since from the start I exclude the possibility that the former recruits more talented persons; I remain with the theory that the leftist cause has created around its nucleus and branches a protective milieu consisting of many organizations (media, universities, culture-groups, literary juries, etc.) which help each other, quote each other's culture heroes, support their own pressure groups, and penetrate influential socio-cultural strata which then carry the message further yet. One could give many, many examples of this basically non-conspiratorial but openly exercised influence, whose effect is to thicken and render impermeable the cultural, religious, academic, psychological environment in which the corruptive ideas and values are nurtured.

It is evident that in order to counterbalance this corruptive influence-network, another network is needed. One that does not keep lamenting over the opponent's successes, does not look for conspiracies and treasons, does not blame the Zeitgeist or bad luck. Instead of all these dead-end streets of speculation, it sets out to organize the counter-offensive: it creates groups of thinkers which lend respectability to the endeavor; sets up a chain of media on various levels and for a diversified public; publishes works of probing spirit and enduring value; calls together congresses where debate is pertinent and of the highest quality; prompts fine intellects to associate among themselves and with the central organs so as to bring about a parallel culture offering an alternative to outsiders: the seekers, the

Korean audience listening to one of the professors' speech

curious, and particularly the legions of those who have been, if not yet irrevocably corrupted by the leftist culture-network, at least aware that they were shortchanged, fooled, misguided and misused.

Needless to say, I do not have a utopian band of rightist ideologues in mind. We do not need to steal ideas from across the very wide avenue which separates us from the leftist ideologues. However, we may "steal" some of their methods which have been the methods of all those who ever organized people and ideas. Now this organization is not a mere view of the mind any more. Thanks to the Reverend Moon and his associates, we have seen in the last decade the emergence of a parallel culture, not rigid but adapting itself to requirements of space and time, yet not so open as to accomodate the latest fad on the market place of ideas. Its success across lands and continents is due to only a few causes. I name first its centering on God without whose help edif-ices crumble. The second cause is the recognition that people have had enough of secularistic, utopian, corruptive ideologies, and seek the positive word. The third is the multi-levelled character of this counter-network, reaching from daily newspapers including *The Washington Times* and *Noticias del Mundo* to the highest levels of scholarship in ICUS, PWPA and the Washington Institute.

This culture-network is not merely another dry academic association. Rather it is a vital group of people committed to positive values and to active promotion of a God-centered world. It is a kind of culture-network that is most needed, standing on solid organizational foundation, and making daily, hourly effort to combat the corruption of utopian ideologies. It is in this that I see the Reverend Moon's achievement, one that makes him such a notable figure of this last quarter of the twentieth century.

The Situation of the World and the Unification Movement

Aleksandras Shtromas

I

The world's most fundamental problem consists in its outdated and totally inadequate political organization. Eighteen hundred nations inhabiting our planet simply cannot reconcile themselves with the world's division into only one hundred and seventy so-called nation states as the sole bearers of internationally recognized sovereignty rights, and they will continue to be restless until national sovereignty is equally distributed among all of them. The movement for equal distribution of national sovereignty encompasses also those nations among the one hundred and seventy in possession of recognized statehood which are either actually deprived of their sovereign rights (as the nations of those formally independent states of Eastern Europe which are under Soviet control) or are artificially divided into separate states as it is the case with Korea and Germany.

Hence, for the world to acquire an adequate political organization, the existing system of one hundred and seventy nation states would have to undergo the process of *fission* (along national lines in multi-national states), *fusion* (uniting single nations artificially divided into separate nation states) and, sometimes, total *reshufflement* (as, for instance, in the case of the Kurds whose homeland, Kurdistan, would have to be carved out from the areas now ruled by Iran, Iraq, Turkey, and the Caucasian republics of the USSR).

This is, however, only one aspect of the problem concerning the inadequacies of the world's political organization. The other and even a more important aspect of this problem is the weakness and in most cases total absence of international political institutions uniting the efforts of the world's nations in attacking problems of mutual concern that can be solved only on a global scale. The most acute among such problems, to name but a few, are the elimination of the danger of nuclear war; the provision of economic aid and means for development; the protection of the natural environment; assistance in alleviating the results of natural calamities and other disasters; regulation of demographic imbalances; exploration and exploitation of the world ocean, international territories (e.g. Antarctica) and outer space; and, last but not least, enhancement and assurance of internationally recognized individual and collective human rights, e.g. the equal rights of all nations. This is to say, that for the world to acquire an adequate political organization, fair distribution of national sovereignty must be accompanied by the creation of new and the enhancement of existing international political institutions embodying and exercising, on behalf of and with the consent of all nations, the sovereignty of mankind as a whole.

II

There are many obstacles that have to be overcome before these necessary changes in the world's political order could become realizable. Among them the most formidable is, no doubt, the present division of the world into communist and non-communist parts. The communists, as an ideological clique single-mindedly committed to the Marxist-Leninist theoretical vision of the world's future, have reconstituted in accordance with that vision the states they succeeded to take over and are seeking to extend the order thus embodied in those states to the rest of the world.

The communist world's relentless activity aimed at creating the universal world order in its own image is in the background of the Soviet-U.S. or, as it is usually called, East-West confrontation. This confrontation has nothing to do with clashing national interests or territorial disputes which simply do not exist between the USSR and the U.S. or any other Western country; it is a purely ideological conflict about the foundations—either communist-totalitarian or liberal-pluralistic, and these are incompatible—on which the universal world order is to be based.

But in the West misconceptions about the nature of the East-West conflict still abound. Because of these misconceptions the West is dealing with the USSR and other communist states as if they were political entities merely dedicated to advance, though in a zealously over-rapacious way, their national-imperial ambitions and thus could be, in principle, that is after being persuaded by means combining deterrence and concessions that this serves their national self-interests best, accomodated within the framework of the pluralistic world order as conceived by the West. That this is a self-defeating policy was clearly demonstrated during the so-called "decade of detente", in the 1970s. None the less, proper conclusions from that experience have not been drawn. The basic Western conception of the communist world has not changed, and, as a result, a new era of misconceived detente is again largely looming on the horizon propped up by false hopes engendered by the youthful image of Gorbachev.

It is a plain fact that the communist world cannot be accomodated into a wider world order framework. By its

very nature, it will be bound to subvert
this framework trying to substitute for it
communist world control. But communist world control would not be able to
provide for a viable world order either.
Wherever communist order was established, it proved to be at variance with
the objective needs of social and economic development and, accordingly,
people's real aspirations and goals. communism on a global scale could hardly
do any better.

On the other hand, communist world
control will most certainly fail to produce a monocentric world government.
Even now the Soviet Union is unable to
control all the communist powers which
were in the first place established and
controlled by it. Moreover, after having
split away from their founding "Soviet
mother", these powers either became
extremely hostile to the Soviet Union—
China and Albania are cases in point—
or, as in the case of Yugoslavia, became
the targets of Soviet hostility. If not for
the powerful presence and containing
influence of the West, the Soviet Union
would have certainly attacked Yugoslavia in 1948 and China in 1969, with
bloody wars ensuing as the result of
these attacks. We have already witnessed
a Vietnamese Communist invasion and
subsequent occupation of an equally
communist Campuchea, as well as a
Chinese communist attack against an
equally communist Vietnam. Just imagine what the situation would be if the
whole world became Communist and no
restraining influence could be exercised
on it from outside. The Orwellian scenario of *1984,* according to which the
three totalitarian communist superpow-
ers are in a constant state of war with
one another, would be beyond doubt
not mere fiction but historic reality. It is

Dr. Aleksandras Shtromas
in Taegu, Korea

unlikely that wars between or among communist powers would be as sloppy as Orwell has envisaged them to be in his novel and that they would proceed along the lines of the present war between Iran and Iraq. It is much more likely that these wars would be fought on a full nuclear scale, and this means that communist world control will most certainly spell the end of mankind.

All this is to say that the only viable political strategy—a strategy assuring the physical survival of mankind and opening its passage into a new, organically peaceful world order—is to eliminate the communist world from the face of the earth and to restore to their proper national selves all nations captured by communism, inclusive of Russia herself. A world with an assured future can only be a world without communism.

By being unable to take proper root in any society and evolve beyond a clique state, communism is a self-defeating force. Therefore it can and should be defeated without war. It is the battle of ideas, not of arms, in which the victory over communism must be achieved. It is also not in confrontation but in solidarity and cooperation with Russia and the other nations subjugated by communism that this battle must be pursued.

To grasp the communist phenomenon in all its complexity it is not enough to be anti-communist. Anti-communism may be as misleading and ill-conceived as pro-communism and can lead to no less wrong conclusions. Only very few people whose voices are heeded worldwide have the profound understanding of communism which is adequate to the real challenge it represents. Among such outstanding people of our time I would single out three, all of whom

lived under communist rule and spent years as inmates of the Gulag, the notorious communist-operated prison camp system which is appropriately named by its victims the system of "labor-extermination camps." One of these three people, along with the great Russian writer Aleksandr Solzhenitsyn and the former Israeli Prime Minister Menachem Begin, is the founder and leader of the Unification Movement, the Reverend Sun Myung Moon.

III

Reverend Moon is a religious leader, and I am not a religious person. Therefore I cannot pronounce any judgments on his religious teachings, the so-called "Divine Principle," or on his ideology of Godism which he counter-opposes to the atheistic counter-religion of Marxism-Leninism. These matters are simply beyond my grasp and outside the field of my main interests.

What, however, strikes me in Reverend Moon as a religious leader is his open-mindedness and tolerance. Differently from most other religions, the Unification movement, far from proclaiming itself to be in possession of the absolute truth, is engaged in the relentless pursuit of knowledge which it tries to gain from a large variety of sources including scientists and scholars like myself, whose world-view is far from being a religious one. This willingness constantly to learn, to build upon its grasp of God's world and will, to listen and draw conclusions for itself without imposing them on anyone else, allows the Unification movement to bring together in the pursuit of truth and meaning people of every persuasion and thus really live up to its name.

To illustrate this, I would like to refer

to one of the very many fields of Reverend Moon's and the Unification movement's work with which I happen to be most familiar. Being gravely concerned about the present precarious state of the world and determined to work for the establishment of a peaceful world order, the Unification movement, instead of launching campaigns or appeals advocating its own specific visions and proposals, founded in 1973 the Professors World Peace Academy in which hundreds of concerned scientists and scholars from over ninety nations, among them world-famous leading specialists in their respective fields, were invited to take part. Scores of national and international conferences discussing relevant topics have since been held, books containing their proceedings published, and series of other books and monographs launched. In 1983 a quarterly academic magazine, the *International Journal on World Peace*, was started and in 1986 *The World & I*, a monthly "thick" (700-odd-pages big) journal comprehensively covering the problems of our changing era, began to appear.

In 1983 a few PWPA scholars, among whom I was too, proposed to hold under the auspices of PWPA a large international conference on the prospects of political change in the Soviet Union and for a post-Soviet world: a topic crucial, in view of the above discussion, to the emergence of a peaceful world order. Reverend Moon agreed to sponsor this conference and the Board of The PWPA-International entrusted me with its organization. I was entirely free in shaping the conference's program and in inviting contributors— paper presenters and discussants. I enjoyed the utmost support for whatever I decided to do from the PWPA's

administrative staff. The conference, which took place in Geneva in August 1985, was indeed a great success. One hundred and fifty leading scholars from the field of Soviet and communist studies took part in it, collectively providing a real breakthrough in our understanding of the problems the Soviet Union faces, the prospects for the Soviet regime's final demise and the alternative regimes that are likely to replace it. A four-volume series of books containing the proceedings of this Conference and analyzing from the point of view of political change every possible aspect of the Soviet system will shortly be published jointly by Paragon House, a New York publishing institution founded by Reverend Moon, and one of the oldest British publishing companies, Macmillan.

It is through such free academic activities which PWPA organizes and sponsors that objective scholarly views on world order problems are gradually forming themselves to the benefit of the academic community, governmental bodies, mass media, the public at large and, no doubt, the Unification movement itself.

PWPA is the venture of the Unification movement of which I am most familiar. There are many others—religious, journalistic, political, educational, cultural, charitable. All of them together aim at helping to bring about a better world—a world based on peace, justice, equal human rights for all individuals and nations. Thousands upon thousands of people from all continents and of all races, religions and professions, most of whom not members of the Unification movement, are brought together and sponsored by Reverend Moon to work for this goal as they deem best. The coincidence of the goals and values of the Unification movement and the amalgamated effort of all these different people is assured by Reverend Moon's commitment to achieve world unity not through uniformity but through the enhancement of the whole variety of the world's religions, nations, cultures and civilizations, all of which in their substance are based on the same belief in God and on efforts aiming at the betterment of man's spiritual and material lot. It seems to me that the slogan of the American nation, "In Pluribus Unum," is also the slogan of the Unification Church. Thanks in great part to the Unification movement's and Reverend Moon's tireless efforts, it may in time also become the slogan of all mankind.

Communism in the Thought of Reverend Moon

Petro B.T. Bilaniuk

There are many different types of anti-communists. Some have become such simply by election or appointment, to fill a position in modern social life. Some have been moved by the love of God and of the free humanity to protect God's interests against the godless and unscrupulous communist authorities and their subversive agencies. And there are those who have been influenced by their scholarly efforts and intellectual endowments to seek the divinely revealed truth and oppose the lies of atheistic communism. Still others have been moved to fight against communism by their aesthetic sense, or by the beauty of religion, church art, worship, religious spirituality, mysticism, and generally the achievements of the spiritual culture of humankind, which are being destroyed and desecrated by communists all over the world. There are also those who have a very keen social and economic consciousness, and work towards peace and social justice within the context of the communist attacks against the free world, its social and economic structures, and its cultural and religious freedom. Finally, there are those who have been forced by adverse political and historical circumstances to become prophets, martyrs, or confessors of the free humanity and religion at the hands of godless communists. These have been called to witness to the Divine Truth and the true humanity by their humiliation, persecution, imprisonment, suffering and blood.

There have been only very few eminent anti-communists, who became charismatics in the field, and who, in their life, work, effort, and suffering, have exhibited all of the above mentioned characteristics of true anti-communists and of the defenders of the interests of God and of the free humanity. In a unique position among them stands the Confessor of anti-communism: the Reverend Sun Myung Moon. A partial record of the life, work and achievements of Reverend Moon which is available to us confirms this conclusion very strongly.

Reverend Moon a Prisoner in North Korea

In June of 1946, in Pyongyang in North Korea, Reverend Moon began his public religious mission. At that time Pyongyang was called by many the "Jerusalem of the East." However the land was under Russian Communist occupation, and Reverend Moon was arrested by the Soviet security forces because of the agitation his preaching caused. In February of 1948 he was sent to a labor camp.

> I served at a communist labor camp for two years and eight months in North Korea. It was a fertilizer factory. Ammonium sulfate powder was carried to the center of the factory by a conveyor belt. The job was to weigh it, put it into bags, then carry them to the freight cars...
> The total rice given in one day was two small bowls, less than full. No pickle. The soup was salt water, not miso soup. We had to work eight hours with such a meal.
> This hard labor was a communist strategy to slowly kill the prisoners. Anyone who went there would die within three years. Without execution. They could eliminate all the prisoners who went to that camp by forcing them to work hard without even a proper meal. In a regular society, people may finish seven hundred bags in a day at most, eating proper food. The quota of the labor camp, however, was double.[1]

Reverend Moon continues his testimony with a bone-chilling account of the life in the communist slave labor camp with vivid descriptions of horrors, humiliation of prisoners, terrible hunger, and brutal murder of the innocent prisoners by their communist guards. There is no doubt that he survived this hell only because of his firm commitment to the love and the Will of God, his invincible faith in God's providence and mercy, and, finally, his service of love to his fellow-prisoners. But the most important aspect of this gruesome experience is described by him in the following words:

> The nearer the completion of the Will comes, the more my heart of gratitude for God increases.
> I never think of any revenge on someone who opposed me, even in my dream. Not at all. If God judged people with that kind of heart, there would be no one remaining on earth. Total destruction would have taken place many thousands of years before. I could never think of revenge on those who hurt my heart.[2]

Needless to say, the experience of Reverend Moon as a communist prisoner and an exploited slave laborer strengthened him spiritually, and helped him crystallize his views concerning communism and how to combat it. Further, nobody can tell him that he does not know what the real practice of communism looks like and how far this practice is removed from the theory of communism destined "for export" to the naive people in the free world.

Totalitarianism

In his analysis of communism, Reverend Moon places it in a broader context of totalitarianism, which he defines as follows:

> Totalitarianism is a political ideol-

ogy which denies the dignity of man's individuality and the freedom of speech, publication, meeting and association, together with the basic human rights regarding the state and the parliamentary system—which are the bases of democratic political ideology of the modern nations—and it insists that any individual or group exists for the benefit and development of the whole nation or state. Therefore, freedom under this system may be defined not as a right for any individual to claim and enjoy, but as a duty or a sacrifice one should pay for the whole.

The guiding principle of totalitarianism does not put any authority on the majority but on one man, the ruler. The will of the ruler, then, becomes the ideology of the whole nation or state.[3]

Dr. Petro Bilaniuk

As examples of the totalitarian political systems, Reverend Moon names those of Mussolini in Italy, Hitler in Germany, and the dictatorial government of the militarists of Japan. However, Reverend Moon also speaks of communism as totalitarianism:

Man is supreme in this physical world. However, the central concept of the communist world denies that man is supreme and tries to enslave man to the one supreme entity which it calls the state. This is a fundamental in the basic principles of the free world and communist world. Under communism all things belong to the Party, which must be obeyed and which has the ultimate goal of world subjugation. Man's value under communism, is exactly the reverse of the value that we advocate in our Principle; communism maintains that a man's value is determined by his loyalty to the Party. Under communism the individual can be sacrificed for the sake of the Party, and in addition the individual can sacrifice everything for the sake of the Party.[4]

In this context, Reverend Moon develops a theocratic counterproposal to totalitarianism, for in a manner of speaking, "all those who pursued goodness throughout history were actually being totalitarian; however, they were absolutely God-centered in their pursuit."[5] He thinks that God allowed communism to spread, in a subtle way teaching mankind to develop a theocratic ideology, that is, a polity with God as its center, as an alternative both to the ideology that exalts individual autonomy and to the ideology that subordinates the individual to a godless state. Thus the Unification Church has the clear-cut goal of transcending individualism, sectarianism and racism and promoting a God-centered polity. "However, the democratic rights of the individual will never be violated in this new ideology."[6]

In this new ideology, there will be no separation of religion and government, for it is not God's will. The true position of religion must be as the center of every aspect of human life. All leaders and civil authorities must be first recognized by God before they are given the mission to govern the society and the world. This is so, for God's sovereignty must be established in this world. The separation of government and religion was never God's will, and it is not a means by which God can fulfill his will. Otherwise the satanic forces would develop unchecked. The United Nations and all civil authorities must be governed not by the civil decisions alone, but by decisions which reflect the will of God.

Dialectical Materialism

Materialism in general is a false theory that physical matter is the only and fundamental reality and that all being and processes and phenomena can be explained as manifestations or results of matter. Out of this doctrine follows quite logically that there is no God, no spiritual world or reality, no religion or need of it. Any social or economic, or cultural change is materially caused. It follows that the only or the highest values or objectives lie in material well-being and in the furtherance of material progress. Dialectical materialism is a Marxian theory that is originally based on the Hegelian dialectics entailing a triad of thesis, antithesis, and a synthesis resulting from the clash of the former two. This theory maintains that the material basis of reality is constantly changing in a dialectical process of thesis, antithesis, and synthesis. From this developed the Marxian theory of historical materialism, which views history and society from purely materialistic and dialectical points of view. Thus ideas and social institutions develop only as the superstructure of a material economic base. Needless to say, materialism, dialectical materialism, and historical materialism form the core and the base of the official communist ideology, philosophy and praxis.

Reverend Moon regards dialectical materialism as the consummate ideological manifestation of the historical forces which deny the existence of God:

Satan, knowing in advance God's providence of giving men this new truth to unify them under one ideology, has set forth a false ideology imitating the true one in his attempt to unify the whole of mankind centering on himself. This satanic "truth" is dialectical materialism. Dialectical materialism attempts to destroy any spiritual being by setting up its own rational ground. The position of this materialism, trying to prove that there is no God, fell into a state of self-destruction, and assumed the logic of denying the existence of Satan himself. Moreover, Satan knows well enough that he himself will perish at the consummation of (evil) history. Realizing his inevitable end, when he will no longer be exalted, he rose to deny God at the risk of sacrificing himself. This denial is actually the core of "dialectical materialism." Therefore, the Heavenly side will never be able to escape from the attack of Satan's theory, unless the democratic world can set forth the truth which will subjugate his ideology. Here lies the historical ground in the providence of restoration that the heavenly side must proclaim the perfect and absolute truth.[7]

Communism in the Light of Old and New Testament Typology

The theocentric or God-centered thought of Reverend Moon looks for types and analogies of the contemporary situation in the history of salvation as recorded in the Bible. The Old Testament typology used by Reverend Moon centers on this fallen world, which is divided into two types: the Cain-type, which is the representative of the Satanic world, and the Abel-type, which is the representative of the Heavenly world, or the Kingdom of God. In reflecting on the great world wars, Reverend Moon teaches that the confrontation between democracy and communism, which he terms the third world war, will be the last war in history prior to the ushering in of the Kingdom of God:

Great world wars are inevitable in order to set up the worldwide condition of indemnity for the restoration of the heavenly sovereignty. If man had perfected himself through the three stages of the growth period without falling, the world under the sovereignty of God would have been realized. Therefore God has to wage the last war to restore the heavenly sovereignty by dividing this fallen world into two types—the Cain-type and the Abel-type—and by having the Heavenly world of the Abel-type smite the Satanic world of the Cain-type, thus restoring worldwide, by indemnity, the act of Cain's having killed Abel. Even in doing that, the three stages must be undergone and thus, three great world wars are inevitable. Therefore, the great world wars are the last wars in which to restore by indemnity, horizontally, the purpose of all the wars that have been waged for the restoration of heavenly sovereignty in the vertical course of the providence.[8]

Reverend Moon also used a New Testament typology of the two thieves crucified on both sides of Jesus in order to examplify the contemporary situation of confrontation between the free democratic world and the godless communist world.

Today, we are aware that Communism is a strong force in this world. The Communists say, "There is no God." And the democratic world or free world says, "God exists." Why do we call the Democratic faction in politics "right," and the Communist faction "left"? Where did this terminology come from? There is an ultimate reason seen from the providential perspective we have been pursuing. This terminology was determined at the time of Jesus' crucifixion. The thief crucified on Jesus' right side forshadowed the democratic world, and the thief crucified on Jesus' left side represented the Communist world.[9]

Then he quotes and comments on Luke 23:39-43 pointing out the noble deed of the right-hand thief, who forgot his own imminent death and defended the innocent Jesus. He continues:

> At that moment the seed was sown by the left-hand side thief that the God-denying world would come into being: the Communist world of today is such a world. And the seed for the existence of a God-fearing world was sown by the thief on the right-hand side. And America is the center of those God-fearing free world nations. America has been chosen as the defender of God, whereas Communism says to the world, "There is no God."[10]

Reverend Moon warns that the communists are completely confident that they can take over churches and use them as their tools. Recent records of the voting in the World Council of Churches confirms Reverend Moon's assessment. Communists have penetrated and infiltrated many church hierarchies, including the College of Cardinals of the Roman Catholic Church. They are promoting some Christian Churches outside of the Soviet Union, for they utilize them as their bases of operation. There are quite a few Christians today, who, being inspired by liberation theology, proclaim that Jesus Christ was the first socialist or even communist, because he blessed the poor and chastised the rich. These "Christian" communists are in fact wolves in sheep's clothing. The story of Cain and Abel repeats itself, but only in a new setting and with new ideologies. All this brings us to the new subdivision of our paper entitled:

Communist Methods of Conquest and Subversion

Communists are quite brutal and vicious, and they don't care what methods they use as long as they accomplish their end. After all, they always subscribed to and practiced their maxim: "The end sanctifies the means to that end."

In their unmistakable goal to conquer the free world, the communists fabricated many lies about outstanding anticommunists. Their principal target has been Reverend Moon. They charged him with a crime of brainwashing his followers and fed this lie to the mass media. They tried to assassinate his character and to discredit him. All this was a part of a much larger plan to infiltrate all religious bodies and organizations. They send their agents pretending to be devout Christians or other believers. These agents give large donations to their respective churches and become officials and leaders, especially of the youth groups. Also, "death of God theology" and "liberation theology" are communist inspired ideologies aiming at the subversion and destabilization of all churches, their theologies, ideologies, cultures, and social structures.

As a result, all of Western civilization is rapidly crumbling, while God-denying people are running rampant, dominating more and more the disintegrating free world. The crucial country in the free world is America, which was given by God Himself a great victory in World War II. Unfortunately, America and the free world are retreating from world responsibility. America is nullifying all of God's victories in World War I and II and the Korean War. Irresponsibly, America isolates itself totally, as the rest of the world falls under communist rule, as seen in Eastern and Central Europe, Cuba, Vietnam, Cambodia, Laos, Ethiopia, Nicaragua, and a host of other countries in Africa, Asia, and South America.

This American failure is due to a lack of a definite objective such as it had in World War II. The Americans must be convinced that they are fighting for the sake of the world in order to protect freedom loving peoples of the entire world. We conclude this observation with a statement from Reverend Moon:

If America does not have a vision of the world and conduct her national business accordingly, how can she be trusted by the world? America must be absolutely clear in her vision. Communism has no place in God's ideal because it denies God. We see very clearly that communism must come to an end and that Godism must take over. The Unification Church is determined and confident to re-educate the communist people. We are not saying that God-fearing people should purge the communists in the way the communists have destroyed their enemies; we must tell them they are wrong and teach them the right way. That is what we are determined to do. I want you to understand clearly why we take this anti-communist position.[11]

Positive Proposals Against Communism

Reverend Moon has often remarked that in order to be victorious over communism one must be superior to them "in God-centered character and in strength of knowledge, experience, and organization."[12] The communists are determined to destroy the free world and take it over. The Unification Church is that force and movement to re-create the world according to the will of God and to liberate the whole world and center it on the true love of God. One step to reach this goal is the home church. Through home church, he envisions a grass-roots revival of moral and religious values that can effectively immunize the people from the enticements of communism.

Reverend Moon also offers a solution to the struggle of the classes in a capitalist society:

According to the logic of Communism, there will be constant struggles as long as there are classes of people. In our ideology, there are no class differences, but only family relationships. Here there is no discrimination. There are no people above or below, but only the relationship between parents and children, providing order in the family.[13]

This solution is quite simple and correct. Marxists of all brands are proclaiming the dogma of their false and materialistic faith that there are classes in the society, and that a classless society is an ideal that must be reached today not by evolution and love, not by conversion of enemies into friends, not by establishing a consciousness of family relationships, but by revolution, blood, and merciless killing of all counter-revolutionaries, especially of the rich capitalists, and ultimately establishment of the dictatorship of the proletariat. They do not seem to notice that this does not lead to the ideal of a classless society, but to a domination of the lowest class over all other classes and to an unjust dictatorial oligarchy, that is, the rule of a few for their own benefit in total disregard of the broad masses of the population.

Finally, Reverend Moon contrasts the communist economic system with his vision of an ideal economy:

The Communist system is for the state, and Democracy is for the individual. We must reach a resolution. The nation which develops that resolution will be the ideal kingdom; it will have the ideal system of economy...

According to Communist ideology, "Mine is mine, and yours is mine." On our part, we must think, "Mine is yours, and yours is the nation's, and the nation's is the world's, and the world's is God's—and God's is mine."[14]

This simple solution is based on love and the correct hierarchy of values established by God Himself. Reverend Moon clarifies this far-reaching statement by a brief thesis concerning his idea of Godism:

In order to fight Communism, we must have the ideology which says that the human beings make one huge family under God as our parent. That ideology cannot be shattered because it is based in divine love as the binding force."[15]

It is impossible in this short paper to exhaust all the riches of Reverend Moon's thought on communism. However, it covers some major points and can serve as an invitation to further study and discussion of this exremely important topic.

Notes

1. Sun Myung Moon, "Testimony", October 13, 1970; unpublished manuscript.

2. Ibid

3. *Divine Principle* (New York: HSA-UWC, 1977) p. 484.

4. Sun Myung Moon, "The Things That Belong to God and the Things That Belong to Man", (May 15,1977, Belvedere, New York) p. 3.

5. Ibid., p. 5.

6. Ibid., p. 7.

7. *Divine Principle*, pp. 492-493.

8. *Ibid.*, pp. 477-493

9. *Sun Myung Moon, God's Warning to the World: Reverend Moon's Message from Prison,* (New York: HSA-UWC, 1985) pp. 88-89.

10. *Ibid.*, p. 89.

11. Sun Myung Moon, "For the Future" (September 10,1978, London, England) p. 12.

12. Sun Myung Moon, "The Completion of the Providence and Parent's Day" (April 15, 1980, World Mission Center, New York)

13. Sun Myung Moon, *A Prophet Speaks Today,* edited by W. Farley Jones (New York: HSA-UWC, 1975) p. 113.

14. *Ibid.*, pp. 112-13.

15. *Ibid.*, p. 113

Towards a Peaceful World with Reverend Sun Myung Moon

Michael R.A. Erdey

Introduction

Throughout the history of man, violence has been his constant companion. Our cave man ancestors might have killed their their neighbors for a fancy sea shell or to possess their wives. Even the Old Testament starts out with a gory scene of human existence on this planet when Cain murders his own brother, Abel, just because his sacrificial offering was favorably received.

Because violence was so much a regular experience of our ancestors, their yearning for peace and harmony was equally strong. From bibilical antiquity to our nuclear age many of us have dreamed about that golden age when swords could finally be converted into plowshares.

Wars are violent and very destructive. Human lives, in their prime years, are sacrificed on the altar of the war god, Mars. Beautiful cities are turned in one day into rubble, ashes and cinder piles. In our age of battleships, airplanes and missiles, the battlefield has moved from the front lines to just about everywhere. There is no more safe haven left for women and little children to hide from the stray bombs and missiles that, accidentally or deliberately, miss a nearby factory, bridge, ammunition depot, microwave communication tower, television or radio antenna, highway junction or railway line that can be found just about everywhere the people are in a modern industrial nation. Thus the yearning for peace in our age is stronger than ever before.

Consequently, so many naive people continue to be easy targets of the well trained professional hucksters and agitators of the Bolsheviks, who disseminate their propaganda under the guise of a peace movement, cleverly posing as the guardian angels of peace and tranquility on earth.

Background Information

I lived for 12 years under the yoke of the Soviet-Russian Bolshevik terror regime, from October 6, 1944, when the drunken hordes of the Red Army arrived in our home-town, till early December 1956, after the Hungarian Revolution was crushed in a blood bath and I arrived in Austria as a refugee.

The Bolsheviks know human behavioral psychology very well, probably better than anybody else in the world. They knew that right after the end of World War II people would do anything to retain their peace. So they told the desperate, homeless, poor and hungry masses that the Bolsheviks want peace, while those dirty capitalist warmongers, who get rich by making weapons and ammunition, want to make sure that the need for their products is perpetuated. So the hammer and sickle, along with the red star, started to appear more and more often together with Picasso's peace dove. Since the forefathers of the Russians grew up in the world of icons, their masters knew very well that symbols presented often together are easily interchanged for each other in the minds of the simple. Thus, the Bolsheviks soon came to be perceived as guardian angels of peace and love in the minds of the European public.

To make certain than their propaganda would not turn the public into pacifists, the Marxist-Leninist seminars that we were forced to attend provided us with additional qualifying statements. We were told that enlightened peace loving should not be equated with the decadent pacifism of those people who are living under the rotten capitalist system. A Soviet citizen has to understand that there are justifiable circumstances under which it is not only the right but also the duty of the people to fight their oppressors, such as:

(a) a War of National Liberation;

(b) a socialist revolution that intends to overthrow the old, rotten social order.

A few notes are here in order. Since it is your duty to support the just side, they have the right to execute you as a traitor if you are aiding the other side in any manner. We have seen what a tremendous advantage the communists had in Vietnam, when they shot on the spot any individual who cooperated with our side in any manner, while our soldiers were only allowed to return fire when they were shot at. Let's also note, if you happened to be among those who get sick and tired of the Bolshevik tyrants and their terror, as have the Hungarians, Poles, East Germans and recently the Afghans, you no longer have such rights. You are now branded a counter revolutionary, who is worthy to be hanged form the next lamp post, if you are caught, of course.

In other words, the Bolshevik value system is a very self-serving one. They will preach peace and appear in the shape of doves and lambs as long as quiet infiltration and propaganda will serve their interest best, but they will suddenly reappear as wolves when the time is right for a violent revolution to overthrow the existing government.

Having been exposed to this cynical and hypocritical ideology for so many years, many times I just don't know whether I should laugh or cry every time I see a misguided nun or priest, together with some fooled Quakers and duped pacifists, marching along, hand-in-hand with communist ideologues, behind a peace dove, the banner of the late, communist, Pablo Picasso.

In this seemingly hopeless situation, when so much of Western opinion was molded by the Bolshevik propaganda machinery with the aid of our leftist news media, when their peace propaganda neutralized almost all the will power to resist communist takeovers around the world, suddenly I was introduced to a true peace organizaton, the Professors World Peace Academy.

Dr. Michael Erdey
speaks in Fukui, Japan

The Professors World Peace Academy
This organization was brought into life by Reverend Sun Myung Moon. Its members come from the academic community irrespective of their race, national origin, sex or religious affiliation. They have only one thing in common: an honest desire to live on a peaceful planet. They meet in international conferences in order to discuss those issues that produce tensions between nations and communities, in order to come up with some good ideas that could either eliminate or minimize the conflict. Some of their ideas and recommendations are also published in the *International Journal of World Peace.* I joined this organization, because there I don't have to parrot slogans handed down from Moscow. Everybody can expose his own thoughts on the vital issues related to human survival on this planet and discuss them with his peers.

Today, when I came here to pay tribute to Reverend Sun Myung Moon, I am laying down at his feet and your feet some of my own thoughts on how to achieve and maintain peace on earth.

Liberty Is Far More Precious Than Peace

John Locke, the English philospher, introduced the idea that we are endowed by our Creator with unalienable rights to life, liberty and property. Through Rousseau these ideas were incorporated into the realm of the French Enlightenment as well. On the American Continent Thomas Paine, Benjamin Franklin and Thomas Jefferson spread the same idea. When Jefferson wrote the Declaration of Independence, he incorporated the rights to life and liberty intact but replaced the property right with the right to the pursuit of happiness.

The Bolsheviks try to ignore that human beings have indeed a preference for their unalienable natural rights over their other needs. They value their freedom so much over peace, that if you take away their liberty, they are even ready to die for it. As long as there are Hungarians, Poles, East Germans, Afghans and others kept enslaved, there will be from time to time uprisings to break the chains and remove the yoke of Bolshevism. Even if every single one of them is crushed, the resultant peace will only be the peace of the prisons, the silence in the GULAG, the quietness of the torture chamber after the last scream of the victim died out, and the tranquility of the cemeteries where the martyrs finally obtain their lasting peace.

Life is the Most Precious Right of Man

Both Locke and Jefferson put our right to life in the first place among our unalienable rights, and we can only agree with that. The right to life in an organized, civilized, human society means the provision of an economic environment that will allow an able bodied human being, having a sound mind, and willing to work, to provide himself and his family with modest food, clothing and adequate shelter. While the Bolsheviks are absolutely ignoring human rights to liberty and property, we in the United States have some shortcomings in the domain of providing a chance for all of out citizens to be able to provide for themselves and their dependent family members the basic necessities of life.

The American welfare system is the biggest disgrace to this formerly great nation. We are producing a large, idle and dependent parasite class in our society. Since this group is increasing daily, along with the related bureaucracy (social workers, administrators, etc.), it provides the welfare politicans with the block votes that keep them in office for life.

Idleness and boredom are conducive to experiments with drugs. The welfare check is not enough to support these habits. The difference is made up with pimping, prostitution, drug pushing and other criminal activities. Since idleness will not produce marketable skills, our welfare population, along with their children, become permantly enclaved to the corrupt welfare system.

A Recommendation to Help Eliminate the U.S. Unemployment and Welfare Problems.

In the United States 42% of the land belongs to local, state or Federal Governments, while one third of this nation's land belongs to the Federal Government alone. On some of the better quality Federal lands we should organize cooperative enterprises for our unemployed and welfare population.

We would give a reasonable amount of time for all recipients to join one of these cooperatives, after which all unemployment and welfare payments will cease.

The cooperatives would be built around as much self-sufficiency as possible. They would not only produce their food but would engage in the most important trades as well. They would repair their appliances and machinery, build and repair their homes, build and repair their furniture. Their members would acquire marketable skills that they could sell on the free market when he opportunity arises and they so desire.

The elimination of the enormous welfare burden would create a real renaissance in our free enterprise sector and an associated quantum leap in our standard of living. Even though the cooperatives would lag somewhat behind them, there would be many who would choose it for one of the following reasons:

(a) They will not require initial skills.

(b) The cooperative gives more security to the timid, the aged, the slow worker, the handicapped, the weak, and those in poor health.

(c) Some will prefer the special services they will provide. Their nurseries and day care services will be preferred by un-wed mothers and large families. Single individuals and working married couples, who don't like cooking, will enjoy their inexpensive food service. Others might prefer their social life and group recreational activities.

(d) There are some religious organizations that prefer communal life-styles. It would also give an outlet for some idealistic socialists to practice what they are preaching within the framework of our system, without the destructive side effects of their dogmas. We could challenge Jane Fonda, the Hollywood advocate of communism, to organize one of the large communes according to her model and show us the results.

The introduction of a mixed economic system having a free enterprise sector along with a communal one would, for the first time in the history of the United States, provide every individual with the true Jeffersonian right to pursue their happiness according to their own beliefs and inner desires. Since this would be achieved with the simulataneous elimination of the welfare system, it would eliminate one of the causes of the flood of illegitimate welfare children, who are presently the burden of the not so willing over-taxed American middle class. Thus, a tremendous social friction would be eliminated from our life. It would at the same time eliminate one of the primary grounds for Marxist agitation, by showing that an enlightened democracy can indeed serve the needs of the poor and hungry.

A Mixed Enterprise System Could Also Serve the Economy of China

It is well known that the communist collective farms have failed miserably.

Because of the enormous size of the U.S.S.R. (more than the U.S. and China combined) and its abundance of natural resources, it can afford to maintain its failing collective farm system and buy grain yearly abroad for its modest population of about 270 million.

The Chinese, on the other hand, have over a billion population and a land area only slightly larger than the U.S., and they therefore could not afford the same luxury. At the beginning of this decade they broke up their communes, and farmers are now allowed to rent family-sized farms. They are required to sell to the state a quota on fixed price, while the remainder they can sell on the free market at their price. This incentive, along with high quality hybrid seeds, has produced a Chinese agricultural miracle during the last few years.

In wheat production alone, China increased its output from 41 million tons to 87 million from 1979 to 1984. The total grain production of China was 407 million tons in 1984, followed by the 312 million tons for the U.S. and only about half as much for the Soviet Union. These figures are especially impressive if we all that China planted 285 million acres in 1984 while the Russian grain acerage was 300 million. Not too long ago China was a famine-stricken nation, but today it has a grain surplus.

In addition to agricultural production, the Chinese have other reasons to introduce a mixed economic system that allows more and more private enterprise to appear parallel to the socialist sector. The first of these reasons is Hong Kong. In order to prevent the outflow of capital from Hong Kong, which currently provides 40% of all of their foreign exchange, before the British transfer it to them in 1997, they promised to retain its economic infrastructure after the take-over. The positive effect of this alone will lead the government to give more freedom to the private sector in the rest of China as well.

Another reason why I believe that China will decide to embark on a mixed economic path is related to its interest to take over Taiwan. The only way it can peacefully annex Taiwan without a bloody military showdown is if it can convince the successful private entrepreneurs of that country that they will not loose after the unification takes place. Since China wants to industrialize, it is to China's advantage for them to keep the life in the booming Hong Kong and Taiwan economies alive. The Professors World Peace Academy could help this reconciliation by holding conferences between the economists, social and political scientists of China, Hong Kong, Taiwan, Korea and Japan.

The success of a mixed economic system in China could also soften its position on Korea in favor of uniting North and South Korea through a democratically elected government and a mixed economic system.

Reducing Tensions Caused by Religion
We should also address those other issues that cause tensions disturbances and bloodshed among our fellow human beings, such as religious, racial, and ideological differences.

In *Pensées Sur La Religion Et Sur Quelques Autres Sujets* (1670), Blaise Pascal stated: "Men never do evil so completely and cheerfully as when they do it from a religious conviction". No year goes by in India without Hindus and Moslems or Hindus and Sikhs killing each other. Problems and conflicts increase in other parts of the world as well with the emergence of the Islamic fundamentalists in the Middle East and Protestant and Jewish fundamentalism in the United States and Israel. All of them have a very self-righteous attitude, that excludes from the domain of God all human beings except those in their own denomination or sect.

This very dangerous trend can be balanced only with another religious movement, one that maintains that all the great world religions are attempts to get closer to God, and that also believes that all human beings with a conscience have a little bit of divine spark in themselves. This is what the members of the Unification Church advocate. In addition, they also believe that eventually all the major religions of this planet will converge and fuse into each other. I have seen the miracles of this movement, first at their religious freedom rallies and later as a participant in their CAUSA seminars. I have seen for the first time in my life not only Protestants and Catholics, but Mormons, Hindus, Buddhists, Moslems and Jews embracing each other and their Unificationist friends as true brothers and sisters.

It is interesting to note that prior to Reverend Moon, India's Mahatma Gandhi expressed similar ideas. So let me quote from Gandhi:

Religions are different roads converging to the same point. What does it matter that we take different roads, so long as we reach the same goal? In reality, there are as many religions as there are individuals.

To Combat Racial Hatred
Racial hatred has provided a prime opening for Marxist agitation. Since the end of World War II, as one after the other of the former colonies obtained their independence, the Bolsheviks have been swarming throughout Africa with guns, ammunition and, of course, with the doctrines of Marx and Lenin. The American leftist news media were sympathetic to these so-called struggles for "national liberation" even when the actual result was mass murder, economic ruin and destruction.

Let's take a case from today's troubled world: the racially polarized South Africa. The Bolshevik-backed African National Congress (ANC) wants a violent revolution to overthrow the present government. In order to generate the right climate, they have to create economic chaos, along with unbearable misery for the masses. When your stomach is full, your dreams are sweet. To assure that the masses have empty stomachs, professsional Marxist agitators and their unwitting allies promote disinvestment in South Africa, in order to bring forth an economic collapse in this former jewel of the African continent. It is unfortunate that the politically misguided Archbishop, Desmond Tutu, is in their hand too. We should have the courage to state that his role is just as catastrophic as the role of those Latin American liberation theologians who helped install the Bolsheviks in Nicaragua. Now blood will flow on the streets like a river, and those brutal Lenin boys with their clenched fists will soak their red flags in the blood of both the innocent and the guilty.

The coming horrors of mass murder, destruction, ruin and misery could have been avoided if the powerful American media would have backed the right people. There is, for example, Dr. Mangosuthu Gatsha Buthelezi, the Chief of the Zulus. He urged moderation, and opposed economic sanctions and disinvestment, in order to find a peaceful solution. Recently even the popular "60 Minutes" TV program tried to ridicule him. The media moguls never tell us that even one of the subordinates of Tutu, Bishop Thomans Stanage, is opposing his disastrous political position. It is no question that the American sensation-hungry journalists will have all the gory details of carnage and massacre, smoldering ruins and cinder replacing former bustling cities. This is what sells their newspapers well.

The South African tragedy could have been prevented with moderation, passive resistance, and a lot of good will and cooperation between the concerned parties. In India, Gandhi has very eloquently shown what these noble human qualities can do in the long run, if people have the patience to wait for the results to materialize. In our age Reverend Moon is doing his best to show us how we can tear down the walls of religious and racial bigotry. In addition to good will, moderation and love, he invokes the help of the Good Lord as well.

How to Deal with Totalitarian Ideologies

As a college student in Hungary, under the iron fist of Stalin, I noticed how easily the blunders of planned economy could have been eliminated by allowing a little more free market to operate. But it was sacrilege under Stalin to even think that Marxism-Leninism isn't perfect.

About the same time, I was taking a course in mathematical logic. There I was introduced to Gödel's famous incompleteness theorem, which states that in consistent, axiomatizable theories there exist formulas that you will not be able to tell whether they are true or false.

Suddenly I felt that here was the explanation why people feel that when they analyze the free market economic system (like Marx), they want to cure it with socialism. But when they see the horrors of the more rigid Marxist system, they immediately want to cure it with capitalism.

The trouble with us human beings is that we want to be purists. We want to see our society either under capitalism or socialism. But the trouble is, either one will have its shortcomings, so you have to mix them. This is why I recommend to solve the economic ills of the United States by adding a dose of communal economy, while prodding China to be a little more open to capitalism. Once both countries admit their shortcomings, then we can shake hands. We should engage totalitarian ideologies in constructive dialogues and draw their attention to the shortcomings of rigid systems. In addition, we should also point to them the enormous suffering caused by the suppression of human liberties.

What I have advocated so far is straightforward, provided that you deal with nations and governments who have some respect for the public opinion of the international community. But what can you do if you deal with a regime, like the Soviet-Russian one, that has enslaved many nations with absolute disregard for human rights and dignity? We must be strong and prepared to defend ourselves. For this reason, I support President Reagan's Strategic Defense Initiative. A strong defense will give us time to try to reduce the tensions around the globe through patient, constructive dialogue.

Concluding Remarks

Peace depends on whether other conditions are satisfied or not. If we want peace, it is a must that our unalienable rights to life, liberty and the pursuit of happiness are not compromised. Interestingly enough, we found that the first and third of these rights are strongly tied to the economic conditions that we as an organized society provide for our citizens.

We also looked at those other conditions that can disturb domestic peace and harmony, such as discrimination due to race, national origin, sex and religious beliefs or ideologies. In these areas we urged patience, tolerance love and understanding towards the wide variety of human values, religious beliefs and ideologies. The non-violent achievements of Gandhi and Reverend Moon demonstrate the right road to peace. Let me cite you once again Gandhi: "In God's house there are many mansions and they are equally holy". I found no good word for the Marxist peace movement, since their ultimate goal is to co-opt naive pacifists and Christian clergy to establish a Bolshevik proletarian dictatorship.

I wanted to make it clear that finally we have a true peace movement, the Professors World Peace Academy, brought to life by Reverend Sun Myung Moon. The membership of this organization comes from all parts of our planet, and addresses real problems that cause tensions and violence in our midst. He gave life to this organization, and now it is up to us to make this organization effective.

As far as Reverend Moon is concerned, I urge you to contact all religious, academic, civic and political organizations to write letters of support in order that he be awarded the Nobel Peace Prize. He is not only the founder of the Professors World Peace Academy, but he and his disciples work so hard through CAUSA and through their daily ministry to promote inter-religious and inter-racial peace, understanding and harmony. So, let's join hands to help this great religious and civic leader of humanity to get this prize that he rightfully deserves, and help him to bring forth a better world for our sake, and for the benefit of our children and the future generations.

SEVEN

PERSONAL STATEMENTS

The Work of Reverend Moon, As I Know It

Frederick Sontag

The general public and the world press know Reverend Moon from one perspective, one that is often quite negative. As the saying goes: "Good news in no news" for a newspaper reporter. Thus, Reverend Moon's religious goals or cultural accomplishments are seldom reported. This, of course, is not unusual; new figures in any field are often treated with disdain at first. It may take a generation for the proper perspective to come into focus on a creative personality.

Each has his own view of Reverend Moon and his work, but mine may be slightly unique. As you may know, Abingdon Press asked me to do a book on the Unification Church and Reverend Moon during the height of the controversy the movement raised in America. In the course of gathering background material, I travelled literally around the world and interviewed hundreds of people, including most of the church leaders and early followers. I always asked, "Who is Reverend Moon to you?" and I got an amazing variety of answers.

As a climax, I ended the book research with a nine hour interview with Reverend Moon, which gave me an unusual insight into the man and his plans. Since that time, I have had an opportunity to be together with Reverend Moon on a number of occasions, which has added to my perspective. I first saw Reverend Moon at an ICUS (International Conference on the Unity of the Sciences) meeting in New York in 1975, so my observations of church activities go back more than ten years.

I joined the board of New ERA (New Ecumenical Research Association), sponsored by the Unification Theological Seminary. I then worked with its board on a project to bring together scholars and theologians from all over the world to discuss God. That was in 1981, and the conference has become an annual event since, producing a whole series of volumes. So far as I know, in its central focus on God this conference is unique.

More recently I have become involved in the board of the Washington Institute, a research "think tank" in the American capital which brings together specialists to discuss all kinds of topics of immediate national and international concern. Before that, I have for over three years been involved in organizing Paragon House Publishers, an international book publishing house Reverend Moon decided to launch in order to provide wider distribution for the scholarly work the conferences produce. The quality of the participants in these conferences has been extremely high, but the written work produced did not get the attention it deserved until we were able to circulate these papers in book form in international publishing circles. Now, Paragon has expanded to become a general publisher of significant works.

Of these enterprises, i.e., ICUS, New ERA, Washington Institute and Paragon House, I have some first-hand and in-depth knowledge. Others will know of a dozen other activities Reverend Moon has pioneered, ranging from commercial fishing, to boat-building, to the Professors World Peace Academy, to newspapers and magazines. The list seems endless and one wonders how these can all be the products of one man's mind and heart. Yet it is true that Reverend Moon is the inspirational source. At least some of these enterprises will not only survive but flourish, forming a monument time cannot erode but can only enhance. And we know the

end is not in sight. New projects arise each day, more I am sure than the energy and talents of Reverend Moon's disciples can carry out in an instant. What can have inspired such diverse cultural activity?

The most commonly asked question I hear is: Why should Reverend Moon do all this? What does he hope to gain, and is there some unseen, ulterior motive behind it all? The answer I find is that what you see is what is intended, that is, a wide variety of cultural activities, always international, always involving prominent people, always aimed simply at cultural benefit. If that seems strange to you, remember that the goal of the church is to speed the coming of the Kingdom of Heaven on earth. Spiritually, God's kingdom begins with Jesus. But, if we are now to make all activities in the world reflect God's wishes, it is important that the church be present on all fronts in society, working to lift it up to God. Thus, each cultural activity is in a real sense an offering to God.

At Reverend Moon's suggestion, I wrote a theme essay for the second God Conference on the topic: "The Defense of God." In this I said that God, and all religious traditions, need defense and that this is our primary responsibility. God expects us to defend, to correct, to improve, every aspect in society as is needed to realize God's purposes. God does not act without us, I believe. Thus, each of the activities of Reverend Moon which I have seen is one more way of defending God, of promoting divine causes, of helping to establish God's kingdom on earth, of bringing secular needs and enterprises closer to God's purpose in creating mankind. To say this is not as subversive to our secular goals as it might seem, since God wants nothing else but the best that can be produced from each human being and every social activity. Our role is to assist cultural improvement.

Lurking in the back of many minds is the suspicion that Reverend Moon "controls" all these activities. In my own experience, this is a mistaken impression. He takes any idea presented to him, or conceived by him, and then usually enlarges upon it. But once it is decided who is going to have the responsibility to develop the project, that person has free reign and full support. The aim is to facilitate projects that improve the well-being of mankind, not to control them.

Dr. Frederick Sontag
in Seoul, Korea

This brings us to the question of Reverend Moon's religious leadership, since the vast series of cultural activities must be seen as one with his religious aims. This is not the time or place to outline all the church's religious activities, but it is enough to say that all the cultural projects grow naturally out of the religious movement. The central aim behind it is to invite people from all races and religious traditions to work together in harmony for the improvement of the human condition.

If God's kingdom and the divine purpose are to reign on earth, how can all human beings be brought together to achieve this goal? Too often religions waste their energy in useless combat with each other. Reverend Moon, I believe, sees himself and his movement as a force enabling differing peoples to work together, to unite in love instead of hatred. Peace and understanding are constant themes in every church venture. How is God's reign to be secured on earth?—that is the constant question and the driving force behind all this activity.

In any account of Reverend Moon's work, one must not forget the spiritual and the pastoral, which I feel is the foundation for everything that is done. Reverend Moon is united with God and wants others to be too. Thus, it is not too much to say that every activity has as its ultimate aim to draw the whole human race closer to God so as to achieve the divine aim. However, it is not enough to do this on a spiritual level only. That is the source of all unity, but the whole structure of family, society, culture and business, must also be brought into harmony with God's plan. This involves drawing new members into the movement, but it is equally important to promote God's plan by entering into every aspect of intellectual and cultural life.

In this way a small number of dedicated followers can accomplish a great deal. Reverend Moon's role is as inspiring source, founder and supporter. By drawing together intellectuals, religious and political leaders, he aims to prove the possibility of reconciliation and cooperation. The unification of the world's religions is the avenue to peace on the cultural and political levels, they believe. The Unification Church is more visible on the public scene than most religious groups, and this is because it is no ordinary church. It is a religious movement that must extend its efforts into all areas of our public life. This is why Reverend Moon's activities spread across the world. At the center is a man called by God for a mission of world reconciliation.

Given the vision and given what has been done, can it all succeed? Really, it does not matter. The attempt is being made; the attempt must be made. Has each project inaugurated by Reverend

Moon succeeded and brought the kingdom of heaven closer to realization on earth? Individually, it does not matter. Like life, if every possible attempt is made, one will succeed and have impact perhaps even beyond the vision which inspired it. It is for us to propose, to attempt to better the world in every possible way; it is for God to dispose, to pick up our effort and make of it what He will. Quite often, other church groups cannot see this plan or accept it. Because Reverend Moon's vision is different and unorthodox, all this sometimes seems like strange activity for a religion, for instance bringing professors from around the world to talk to you. Can we see the whole of God's plan and discern the principle guiding these many activities?

Is it not the case that at different times in different circumstances God has worked differently with different peoples and individuals? The question is: who can discern the principle behind God's action in the present day? And, what activity on our part will carry that plan to greater fruition? I believe we find God's activity embodied in different individuals in different times and places, not in just one or in one unchanging plan. God may be more flexible in His plans and in choosing His instruments than we imagine. What we need to do is to study the major religious and cultural figures of our day, looking always for a sign of God's activity.

But are we always as perceptive as we should be in discerning God's activity at the time? Or, does religious history show us that often only a few can see through the confusion of the hour and discount the hostility which novel views always seem to generate? Most can only see what God has done when they look back in later years. If God never appears directly but always uses instruments, this is not unimportant, becuase then, to an undiscerning eye, one will see only a man or woman, secular or profane, never the presence of God. Like Jesus in his time, few could see what his program was, other than that it was disturbing to conventional ways. We too easily remain closed to new perceptions.

What can be done to open our eyes to see how and where God operates in our time? This is a hard question, and it has no easy answer. And perhaps it has no one answer that can serve for all people. Whom, then, shall we follow and to what activity should we devote ourselves in order to help liberate the human race from its bondage? New movements in religion have always arisen in unexpected places. Become acquainted with the scope of Reverend Moon's activities. Study to understand the vision he offers you for the future, and then decide for yourself if you see God's hand moving there. Making a venture in religious commitment is the only way we can move forward.

God Is Blessing
The Reverend Moon

Joseph C. Paige

I am not a stranger to Korea. I was here as part of the United Nations Command forces during and after the Korean War. I fought here, and I was injured here. I came here to help fight communist aggression, and I am glad that I did. I have continued to fight against communism since that time.

One of the major appeals of Reverend Doctor Sun Myung Moon and the Unification Movement, at least to me, is their strong anti-communist position and the desire to promote Godism worldwide as an alternative to sin and the evils of the world.

I am told by some of my friends in Europe and in America that the communists fear Reverend Moon more than they fear some of the most respected nations of the West and their leaders. This says a lot to me, as I am sure that it does to you.

As I am sure many of you know by now, I am intimately associated with Reverend Moon and the Unification Movement. I have studied the dynamic history and revelations of this great world leader and this great movement. I am familiar with Reverend Moon's visions, the revelations by God to him, and his continuing struggles and his triumphs.

I am persuaded that God is using Reverend Moon and the Unification Movement for the purposes of restoration and Kingdom building. I have studied the Divine Principles, and while there are some legitimate differences between some of the Christology of Unificationism and mainline Christian thought, the central truths, to me, and what I consider more important, is that we are mutually agreed on who God is, that Jesus is the Son of God, and that Jesus is Lord of the world.

Dr. Joseph Paige

The fact that the Unification Movement reaches out to all of the religions of the world—Christian and non-Christians alike, under the "God" banner, also, has major appeal.

I am inspired by the great work that Reverend Moon is doing, not just in Japan, Korea and America but worldwide. I know God is blessing his efforts.

As a black American Professor, educational administrator, minister, social and political activist, it is easy for me to relate to the Unification Movement, for we see so much of Reverend Moon's courage and determination to correct social and political evils and wrongs as kin to that of the great American civil rights leader, the late Dr. Martin Luther King, Jr.

At the Shaw Divinity School, we have had some first-hand relationships with Reverend Moon and the Unification Movement. And I can say truthfully and with pride: God has blessed our involvement with, and our recognition of Reverend Moon and the Unification Movement, and God is continuing His blessing.

You might recall that the Shaw Divinity School was the first mainline institution of any kind in the United States to honor Reverend Moon. We awarded him an Honorary Doctor of Divinity Degree on May 10, 1985. We did this while he was still incarcerated in the Danbury Prison. We did this against all odds, and against pressures by a significant segment of the religious community in the United States and the world not to do so. Yet we knew that in honoring Reverend Moon, we were acting in the spirit of Jesus Christ. We knew that God would be pleased with our action. Mrs. Moon came to our campus and accepted the degree for Reverend Moon.

Many people predicted that the awarding of the degree would be the end of Shaw Divinity School, and that we would be forced to close our doors before December of 1985. But that did not happen. I am pleased to say to you today that God blessed our effort. I know now, as I did then, that our honoring Reverend Moon was God oriented and God directed.

Last year, the Shaw Divinity School had the best year since its founding. Our enrollment was the highest, ever. We raised more money and spent more money than at any other time in the history of the Divinity School. We brought in two new full-time faculty persons. In addition, we increased our library holdings. To top all of the above, just recently, on June 17, 1986, we were granted membership to the Association of Theological Schools in the United States and Canada (ATS), the official accrediting agency in North America.

I could go on and on in witnessing to the goodness of God and His blessings that are ours which we credit almost wholly to our relationship with the Unification Movement.

Of course, we give God the glory!

May God continue to bless you, your friends and counterparts in Korea and Japan.

I know that the Professors World Peace Academy and the professors of the world are very dear to Reverend Dr. Moon. Like him, I know professors figure prominently in God's providence for Japan, Korea, the Far East, the Middle East, Europe and the Americas. I am proud to be part of this great gathering. I know that I will return to America more inspired.

Ours is a great challenge, and we shall overcome.

Reverend Moon:
A Visionary
For Peace

Betty Rubenstein

An American woman of modest accomplishments speaks to you today because of the vision of one man who came to my country to pray and work for peace. That man is Reverend Sun Myung Moon. His imaginative vision, which I believe comes from God, is broad and inclusive. All humankind dreams of a peaceful world, but few have found as many ways to bring that vision into fruition; to make a sound and practical contribution.

Some of us have endured criticism for our activities connected with the church, but gradually, as the saying goes, *"By their fruits you shall know them,"* the work has become respected and the criticism has begun to wear away. Of course, with success comes some jealousy. And Reverend Moon's projects have been successful.

My first experience with Reverend Moon was at an International Conference on the Unity of the Sciences (ICUS), at which Reverend Moon annually invites scientists from all over the world to share their knowledge. There, gathered in one conference were professors from every major discipline—scientists, historians, sociologists and artists, people from the Orient and the Middle East as well as Western scholars—all seeking to transcend the narrow confines of their campus life to discuss and work for a vision of world peace. In addition to the learned discussions, these meetings of scholars have created a network around the world of people of different faiths who respect each other, who develop understanding between people. This increases the chances for peace in a very real way.

But it was only when I went to Reverend Moon's seminary for the graduation of his theological students that I began

Dr. Betty Rubenstein
is greeted in
Kyoko, Japan

to understand the depth that lies behind these projects. When he prayed, his prayer—though I couldn't understand the Korean language—touched the depth of my heart. It was clear Reverend Moon saw the need to bring people together in freedom as the way to God. I learned of his prophetic foresight and agenda for development: (1) to bring the world's religions together, (2) to fight communism; (3) to return young people to a moral life.

After ten years, I realize Reverend Moon is not only a *visionary theologian,* he is also a *visionary economist,* who can direct international enterprises for the goal of peace, not just profit (although, of course, the business must be sound).

He is a *visionary sociologist,* who brings whole groups together who suffer from national and racial prejudice. Americans come to Japan, Japanese go to Korea, Koreans travel around the world, all at the inspiration of Reverend Moon.

But he is also a *visionary politician.* I have learned about Japan's recent election in which the International Federation for the Victory over Communism (IFVOC) worked hard to win a victory for the LDP. The the work of IFVOC is important because communism is a world-wide threat to peace. Reverend Moon understands this, and in all these ways—theological, sociological, economic, and political—he finds active ways to further the cause of peace.

It is my opinion, after being a friend of the Unification Church for ten years and sharing in many of its projects, that Reverend Moon works miracles for peace. Time after time, he announces a project which seems impossible—too big, too grand. A few years ago, he decided to send one hundred young people on a religious pilgrimage to visit holy places around the world. I thought this would never work, but it did, and the Youth Seminar on World Religions (YSWR), a continuing project, is the enormously successful result. Hundreds of young people have had their narrow vision expanded. When they take their places in their own countries they will have the consciousness of world citizens, a requirement of the modern situation.

When Reverend Moon decided to publish a newspaper in Washington D.C., I thought this was just dreaming. But Reverend Moon believed that the capital of the Free World was not adequately served by the left-leaning *Washington Post*. He thought the *Washington Post* did not fully understand the crisis of world communism. So he created the *Washington Times,* a well written, accurate newspaper. I was sure the paper would fail. Who would read a newspaper sponsored by the Unificaion Church? Now, the President of the United States, Ronald Reagan, reads the *Washington Times* every day and says it is his favorite paper.

I am on the board and have taken part myself in conferences of the New Ecumenical Research Association (New ERA), sponsored by the Unification Church. This body brings academics together from all of the world's religions to exchange ideas about God and spiritual life. Since my field of research is Art and Religion, I contribute papers to the God Conference which examine the ideas behind religious architecture, painting and sculpture.

For example, I have written about the Ise shrine in Mie Prefecture, Japan, and compared it to St. Peter's Cathedral in Rome, explaining that the differences in building style illustrate the differences in the two cultures East and West. The setting of the Ise shrine, deep in the woods, surrounded by three wooden fences, embodies, as you know so well, many principles of Japanese culture. Every effort has been made to stay close to nature. By rebuilding the shrine to the founding Sun goddess Amaterasu-o-mi-kami every twenty years, the most archaic memories of Japan are kept fresh and vital.

What a contrast this Imperial shrine makes with the central shrine of world Catholicism. Instead of hiding secretly in the woods among the sweet smelling cedar trees, the great dome of St. Peter's, designed in the sixteenth century by Michelangelo, rises high, dominating the skyline of Rome and calls attention to the power of the church. As one approaches the building, huge colonades of marble pillars designed by Gian Lorenzo Bernini throw their arms wide to embrace hundreds of thousands of pilgrims, whose goal is to enter the church and worship at the grave of St. Peter who lies buried beneath a great altar. St. Peter's basilica is a tribute to the ability of man to shape space to his own purposes. Four centuries of Italian artists have contributed works to adorn the inside of this building. Christianity, in contrast to Japanese culture, is an indoor religion. Nature is forgotten and the works of man are dedicated to God.

Nowhere is the contrast of cultures seen as clearly as in the difference of these two buildings, Naiku at Ise and St. Peter's in Rome. The strengths and weaknesses of both cultures are apparent. Western man, in his hurry to change the world, is in danger of ruining it. The Oriental world, in its love of tradition, its training in Confucianism, Buddhism and Shinto, is in danger of too great a love for the past and too rigid a hierarchical structure which can sometimes stifle achievement and the spirit. Reverend Moon likewise sees the strengths of both systems. He is trying in very important ways to bring East and West together.

I have also discussed the religious ideas behind the paintings of Marc Chagall, a Jew who designed stained glass windows for Catholic cathedrals. His works contain images from the Old and New Testaments, united in a mystical way. In my opinion, the terrible events of World War II made it impossible for Chagall to remain within his own faith tradition. His spirit was too all-inclusive. He saw God's message in a broader concept, as does Reverend Moon.

I am currently preparing an essay on Japan's famous painter, Higashiyama Kaii, for one of the newest visionary projects of Reverend Moon, *The World & I* magazine. This magazine contains beautifully illustrated articles on history, religion, politics, philosophy and art. When I heard the magazine was going to have 700 pages, once again, this seemed as impossible as the other projects, but I was wrong again. The magazine is world-wide in its scope and is dedicated to a vision of the unity of mankind. Even holding the magazine in the hands is a pleasure and one more indication of the great concept behind it.

In 1984 and 1985, I was on the planning committee for the Assembly of World Religions, one of the delegates from twelve religions who came together to plan a large assembly for November, 1985. The plan was to invite ministers and laymen from every religion would join in a religious gathering, where spiritual matters could be freely and openly discussed and where each group could pray in its own manner.

The planning committee worked diligently. But we would always say to each other, "Can this really happen?" We were scared that all our plans were imagination and not reality. But the man behind the vision had faith that it would come to pass. Today, all over the world there are 800 or more people whose spirit was touched by having attended this great Assembly. Hindus and Buddhists, Jews and Christians, Native Americans and Africans, Sikhs and Taoists, Jains and Zoroatrians, Eastern Orthodox believers, all came together to share their religious heritage and diverse legacies of faith.

I have learned slowly never to say, "Reverend Moon will never be able to do that!"

One last word of my own personal observations of Reverend Moon. I have met him in good times and difficult times. When Reverend Moon testified before the United States Senate committee in connection with the false charges raised against him, he was calm and strong in spirit. He met the adverse court decisions with the same strength. I was at the reception at the Washington Press Club when Reverend Moon came out of Danbury Prison. He was the same strong, visionary person. He did not ever complain. He did not utter one bitter word at the injustice done to him. He seems to me to be so close to a higher level of consciousness that he can live the life of an ordinary person, a husband, a father, a teacher, and at the same time be in touch with energies from somewhere else. He gives everyone around him strength drawn from that transcendent source. Even in prison, there are stories and tales of his inner strength that are amazing: He would be the first to finish his work, and then he would help others. Late into the night and early in the morning he could be found at prayer... I know church members who don't sleep very much either. Something of Reverend Moon's energy touches them, and they work for peace around the clock.

It has been my privilege to be in Reverend Moon's presence under many differing circumstances. He is always strong and kind, and also sometimes full of fun. I have heard him sing and heard him pray. I have heard him speak with strength and force as well as with gentleness. In my opinion (and remember I am not a member of the Unification Church, only a good friend) Reverend Moon is a holy man. He is a holy man with the breadth of vision that is genuine, deep and broad. Together with his wife, family, his church members, and the many thousands of professors, religious leaders and lay people who support his projects and count themselves his friends, there is a better chance that all humanity will breathe in peace.

My Views on the Endeavors of the Reverend Sun Myung Moon

Teshome G. Wagaw

In the early part of winter 1985 I received a telephone call from a reporter of one of the major newspapers of Michigan. The caller, after identifying herself, wanted to know whether I knew that my name was listed as one of the supporters of the Reverend Sun Myung Moon, and whether my employer, the University of Michigan, was aware of this. She said the founder of the Unification Movement is very controversial and in view of that what was I doing by associating with such movement. My response to her was that I knew what I was doing and that whether my university's administration knew or not is totally irrelevant to me, and as far as controversies are concerned I would have been more surprised if they were absent. I told her that a reading of history would inform us no great movement, religious or otherwise, was immune at the beginning at least to misunderstandings and even persecution. Just think of the founder of Christianity and his early followers. They were insulted, persecuted and eventually Christ, along with some of his followers, was put to death. That pattern to a varying degree repeats itself throughout history.

Clearly the journalist, for her own reasons, was trying to intimidate me. But upon my assertive statements in the affirmative she cooled down and said goodbye. There were other similar inquiries I get from time to time, mostly from fellow academicians. They tell many stories how the movement's leaders did this and that and how some young people were forced into accepting teachings of the Unification Church by coercive methods and so forth. I respond to such innuendoes simply by stating that based on my understanding

Dr. Teshome Wagaw
and his party visiting
the Japan Alps

of the philosophy of the movement, such accusations could not hold water.

Bear in mind that although I am a practicing Christian, I am not a member of the Unification Church. But to the extent that this church espouses some philosophies that touch the cords of my humanity and my religious as well as ethical values and convictions, to that degree I will support it in its activities as best as I can.

What are some of the underlying principles espoused by the Reverend Sun Myung Moon's movement that are appealing to me? As I understand them they are the following: the search for eternal truth; a love for fellow human beings; and the search to establish a world based on justice and goodness. These principles are in full accordance with the teachings of the Old and New Testaments of the Bible as well as the tenets of other religious teachings. There is one difference in the case in point. After enunciating these principles, the Reverend Moon did not stop there. He went ahead in his own time to implement them by creating a number of organizations specifically designed to address defined areas of global and human concern. Some of these organizations that I am more familiar with include the International Conference on the Unity of the Sciences (ICUS), the Professors World Peace Academy (PWPA), and Paragon House Publishers.

These endeavors are concrete manifestations of the vision of the Reverend Moon. The participants include some of the outstanding minds of the world, and the deliberations are often of the highest order. The organizers, usually drawn from the staff of the various branches of ICF, are competent, patient and understanding. One often hears participants remark that the forums afforded under the umbrella of ICF are the best of their kind in the world. Even the United Nations does not approach the quality and efficiency afforded by ICF. All these costly activities have one fundamental aim: that is world progress in peace, justice, human dignity and brotherhood. Many others often talk of such principles. But in the case of the Reverend Moon they are given concrete expression.

I believe that, in his present stage, man needs to rely on religious values. He needs noble ideas and ideals to strive toward. Man needs to realize the noblest ideals that inspire and guide human thoughts and actions in relation to man himself, his family, his community, his nation, and indeed the larger cosmos. I believe it is only in this context that man can make genuine progress towards the realization of making himself truly and productively humane, loving, kind, and understanding.

Another point that inspires my confidence, and hence full support and participation in the endeavors envisioned by Reverend Moon, is that his programs have room enough and are secure enough to invite people of divergent points of view and persuasions to participate.

In contrast to other similar movements, this one believes and practices genuine international, ecumenical dialogues among people of divergent beliefs and persuasions. I believe this is the way to address the most fundamental, the most pressing issues of the world today arising from the environmental, economic, military and political problems. I am further persuaded that as long as there are enough people in the world who are willing and able to summon all their human and material resources to address pressing problems, there will be hope for peaceful resolutions for the many conflicts of society.

Human history is fraught with conflicts, wars, persecutions, exploitations of the weak by the strong, and much too much destruction. Unless humanity follows a different course the next world conflict will be the last for human beings to survive.

Some people, usually Westerners, get upset when their son or daughter gets involved with the Unification Movement. They seem to say that this movement, or some of its practices, are alien to their way of thinking or to their religion. But what they and people like them seem to forget is that all great religious movements of the world have been considered as alien when they began. The leaders and the followers of such movements have been often severely persecuted, or even killed. Furthermore, let it not be forgotten that all of the great religions of today were founded in Asia by Asians, and not in the West as many seem to think. Moses, Mohammed, Jesus, and in our own time Mahatma Gandhi, all were Asians. It is altogether possible that another movement, led by an Asian, Reverend Moon, is in the making today. Perhaps this time such a movement would have come, as did others in their own time, in response to the acute needs of the time; needs such as international peace among nations, equal justice and freedom for all, and brotherhood and love among the large spectrum of the human race. Who is to say such an embracing movement is not in the making at this time?

To the extent that the visions and

actions initiated by Reverend Moon contribute to the happiness and prosperity
of a peaceful world, they deserve the
fullest support by the most thoughtful
members of human society.

APPENDIX

Four Steps
To Absolute Peace

Hisatoki Komaki

Dedicated to
The Reverend Sun Myung Moon

"God created man to be the ruler
of the universe."
Reverend Sun Myung Moon, *Divine
Principle*

It is my most urgent duty to correct
my two essays on "Four Steps to Absolute Peace" in *The New York Times* of
June 15, 1986, and July 6, 1986. Unfortunately, when I wrote these two important essays, I knew nothing about the
Divine Principle of Reverend Sun
Myung Moon.

On July 29th, 1986, only one month
later, I was so fortunate as to come to
know the Divine Principle (Unification
Theology) through Professor Betty Rog-
ers Rubenstein's academic lecture at the
Karasuma-Kyoto Hotel in Kyoto. It was
my new birth. (Oh, "July 29, 1986" is
my new birthday.... Yes, on July 29,
1986, I was newly born!)

My "Four Steps to Absolute Peace"
(condensed in *The New York Times Book
Review* section from my *Selected Works*
(in English and in French, vols. I, II,
III, IV), may be summarized as follows:

Goal I. Complete World
         Disarmament.
Goal II. Phasing Out of the Killing
         of Higher Animals.
Goal III. Phasing Out of Accidental,
         or Internecine Killing of
         Small Animals (Insects,
         etc.)
Goal IV. Permanent, Rapid, and
         Smooth Salvation of All
         Sentient or Psychic Beings
         (including psychic beings
         higher than humankind)
         of the Visible and Invisible
         Eternal Universe from
         Severe Pain.

I think that Goals I, II, III and IV
are quite right. I feel, however, it is my
most urgent duty to correct my essays
on the *method* of how to attain these.
When I wrote my two essays, unfortu-

nately, I knew nothing about Reverend Sun Myung Moon's great, perhaps the greatest, epoch-making theology. Now that I have come to know Reverend Sun Myung Moon's theology and his social movement (International Federation for Victory over Communism), it becomes my urgent duty to correct my two essays upon my new theoretical foundation: the firm basis of Reverend Sun Myung Moon's great epoch-making thought for true peace of all creatures of the universe.

My two essays may be summarized as follows:

Goal I.   Complete World Disarmament (World Federation)

In the June 15 issue, I wrote:

...the USSR has proposed complete world disarmament already. I sincerely hope that, at the nearest chance, the U.S. President would accept this USSR proposal, with a practical schedule that the top leaders of both the US and the USSR can accept...

It was a terrible mistake. Now, I must correct my proposal as follows:

Only through Reverend Sun Myung Moon's great theology and his "Victory over Communism" movement, will true peace come on the Earth, and, consequently, complete world disarmament, along with a World Federation, will be realizd very soon... on the firm foundations of V.O.C. and CAUSA...

Goal II.   Phasing out of the Killing of Higher Animals

Goal III. Phasing out of the Accidental, or Internecine Killing of Lower Animals (Insects, etc).

Goals II and III, are problems to be solved by the biological sciences, including, of course, bio-technology.

In his Founder's Address to the First ICUS, New York, 1972, Reverend Sun Myung Moon stated: "As repeatedly mentioned, man has come to reflect God's creativity through outstanding scientific progress, but so far has not learned His love."[1]

Goal II phasing out of the killing of higher animals—is very easy to approach and has been discussed in such publications as *Vegetarian* magazine, UK, or *The Vegetarian Times* magazine, USA. Goal III—phasing out of the accidental or even internicine killing of lower animals like insects—may be very difficult to approach. Of course, in our experimental farm, we do not use any insecticides.

Goal IV. Eternal Happiness of All Existential Beings of the Infinite Universe (Permanent, rapid and smooth salvation of all "existential" beings of the universe from severe pain.)

In the July 6, 1986 issue of The New York Times, I wrote:

According to Christian theology, Goal IV can be attained only through the sincerest prayer of all humankind via Christ Jesus, the Second Person of the Absolute Causal Being, warranted by the fulfillment of the Biblical prophecies, who died and was resurrected *not only* for humankind *but also* for the eternal happiness of all creatures—all 'existential' beings—(including, of course, the intellectual beings higher than humankind of this and other worlds.[2]

According to the Nichiren Shoshu Buddhist philosophy, Goal IV can be achieved only through a powerful chanting of "the phonetic and ideographical expression of Cosmic Mercifulness; (*nam myo ho renge kyo*) in front of a Mandala of Taisekiji." This is Buddha's most merciful prayer for the rapid achievement of the eternal happiness of all existential beings of this and other worlds—the eternal and infinite universe.

I sincerely hope that all civilized people *move* for I, II and III, and *pray* for IV.

These are the summaries of my two essays on "Four steps to Absolute Peace: Man and Other Creatures are Brothers and Sisters". One month later, I was so fortunate as to come to know Reverend Sun Myung Moon's true pacifism.

In his Founder's Address for the first International Conference on the Unity of the Sciences, Reverend Sun Myung Moon taught us:

> From the standpoint of ontology, the cosmos is a world of effect and it must therefore have an ultimate cause. Materialism says this ultimate cause is matter and idealism insists that it is spirit. However, because the world of effect is made of unified beings with two natures, the cause must also be a monistic being with the potential of the two natures of matter and mind unified into one.[3]

He also teaches us, "The essence of God (or Eternal Being) is heart."[4] In Nichiren Shoshu Buddhism, the Eternal Buddha (Absolute Causal Being)'s most merciful *heart* is expressed as the Taisekiji mandala: *nam myo ho renge kyo*. In Catholicism, the Absolute Causal Being's most merciful *heart* is expressed as the Most Sacred Heart of St. Mary. This God (the Eternal Buddha or Absolute Causal Being) is the unified being which is the fundamental cause of the cosmos. "Then how could God create the cosmos", including all other creatures and man? According to Reverend Moon," God (Absolute Causal Being) could do it because God has *heart*.... God's goal of creation is to have man and world (all creatures of this and other universes) of eternal happiness, that is the Kingdom

of Heaven, reflecting the love and creativity of God, which relate mind and matter respectively."[5]

Therefore, all beings are meant to be unified. Man is a unified being of body and reason or mind; animals are the unified beings of body and instinct, capable of feeling severe pain; and plants are the unified beings of matter and directive life force, without any sensation of pain. Because God, the Absolute Causal Being, is a unified being with a most merciful heart, man and and other creatures of the universe should also be unified.

More accurately expressed, God (the Eternal Buddha; the Absolute Causal Being) created man to be the ruler of the universe (Gen 1:28). God created man to be the mediator and the center of harmony of the universe. Unfortunately, however, because of the fall of man, the whole creation (the universe) lost its ruler. In his *Divine Principle*, Reverend Sun Myung Moon states:

> Because of the fall of man, however, the whole creation lost its ruler. We read in Romans 8:19 that the creation waits in eager longing for the revealing of the sons of God (restored men of the original nature). Romans 8:22 continues with, 'the whole creation has been groaning in travail together'. This is because the give and take action between the visible and invisible worlds has been cut off due to the fall of man...[6]

This is the conclusion. This is the conclusion of conclusions! This is the true answer to my "Goal IV."

Only through the fulfillment of God's third blessing — I assume that God's third blessing (paradise on the earth) includes the fulfillment of the "give and take" action between men and animals on this planet earth (II and III)—can

God's "fourth blessing", namely the perfection of all spiritual beings and God's direct dominion upon the spirit man as the ruler of all creatures of the visible and invisible universe, be put into practice. Then, "The permanent, rapid, and smooth salvation of all sentient and psychic cratures of the visible and invisible worlds from severe pain"—my "Goal IV"—will be fulfilled completely.

For this is the very Purpose of God (Eternal Buddha; Absolute Causal Being) in creating man and all of the visible and invisible worlds.

So I conclude that only through the promulgation of Reverend Sun Myung Moon's Divine Principle, can my Goals I, II, III, and IV—all four of my "Four Steps to Absolute Peace" published in *The New York Times*—be put into practice.

For myself, as a Catholic, a Life Member of the Catholic Study Circle for Animal Welfare (United Kingdom), as well as an university professor of theoretical biology, this means to introduce the Unification Theology into the Catholic Theology (and Unification Theology is completely biblical) and to apply Unification Thought in theoretical biology. This is the very reason why I made up my mind to become a member of the Unification Movement here in Japan.

In conclusion, I would like to make a proposal. Let us do our best to achieve Goal I—Complete world disarmament or a World Federation—through the "Victory over Communism" movement. Let us continue to lend our creative efforts to toward achieving Goal II—Phasing out of the killing of higher animals, and Goal III—Phasing out of the accidental or even internecine killing of lower animals like insects, because "man has come to reflect God's creativity

through outstanding scientific progess". Finally, let us *act* and *pray* for Goal IV—Eternal happiness of all existential beings of the infinite universe through permanent, rapid and smooth salvation of all 'existential' beings of the universe from severe pain.

Someone may say: "Is Goal IV possible?" I would like to answer: "It is quite possible, because man and the universe are unified as one." "God created man to be the ruler of the universe"; therefore, absolute peace among men will bring the realization of the eternal happiness of all existential beings.

In his Founder's Address to ICUS X (Seoul, 1981), Reverend Sun Myung moon gave us four goals as follows:

> In conclusion, Korea has to accomplish four great tasks centering on the Unification Movement. They are: First, a unity of religions through an ecumenical movement; second, a unity of thought by overcoming materialisic communism through a "Victory over Communism" movement; Third, a unity of culture by establishing a new lifestyle in which the cultures of the East and the West are combined; and Fourth, a unity of economy through a new ideology.[7]

I completely support Reverend Moon's four proposals as tasks not only for Korea but for the world. These four proposals must be achieved within the 20th century. And, after that, I sincerely hope that my proposal on the "Four Steps to Absolute Peace" will be achieved within the 21st century.

In concluding my humble paper, I would like to read from Reverend Sun Myung Moon's Founder's Address to ICUS III (London, 1974):

> The discovery that a dolphin can communicate with human beings intelligently deserves notice. Along

the same lines, it has been observed that plants respond to the love and other emotional states of human beings. These discoveries suggest that our present view that the animal and plant worlds are lacking in consciousness and reason may be limited. We may now as well envision a universe in which a harmonious co-existence may be brought about between human beings and other creatures, where man, being the center of all things, may serve as the spokes of the wheel turning the whole universe in ultimate harmony and oneness.[8]

This will realize, for the first time, the true value of human life. It will make possible, the longed-for absolute peace as the proper condition of our spaceship earth.

Notes

1. Sun Myung Moon, *Science and Absolute Values : 10 Address by Sun Myung Moon* (New York: ICF Press, 1982), pp. 9-10
2. cf. Paul Davies, *Other Worlds* (London, Toronto and Melbourne: J.M. Dent and Sons).
3. Sun Myung Moon, *op. cit.*, p. 5
4. *Ibid.*, p. 8
5. *Ibid.*, pp. 8-9
6. *Divine Principle*, (New York: HSA-UWC, 1977), p. 59
7. *Science and Absolute Values*, pp. 100-101.
8. *Ibid.*, pp. 24-25